GLIMPSES THROUGH THE DARK GLASS

CHRISTIAN MEDITATIONS FOR LENT

LARRY D. POWELL

C.S.S. Publishing Co., Inc.

Lima, Ohio

Library of Congress Cataloging-in-Publication Data

Powell, Larry D., 1939-
    Glimpses through the dark glass: a Lenten reader / Larry D.
Powell.
        p.   cm.
    ISBN 1-55673-167-1
    1. Lent--Meditations.   I. Title.
BV85.P69   1990
242'.34--dc20   89-39111
                                                                    CIP

9014 / ISBN 1-55673-167-1   PRINTED IN U.S.A.

CONTENTS

"For now we see through a glass darkly . . ."
1 Corinthians 13:12 (KJV)

Foreword

When the United Methodists of Arkansas were asked what they liked best about their state newspaper, the two things mentioned first were the Bishop's column and the Sunday School lessons.

For several years now, Rev. Larry Powell has written the lessons for the denominational paper. They are simply written, easy to read, and easy to understand. But a regular reading of them reveals the scholastic background that the Rev. Mr. Powell brings to them. It is obvious that he studies, and thinks, and translates what the Bible means to him and how it fits and works in today's world.

He writes of faith and love and commitment. He researches the history of the Biblical passages, provides illustrations that bring them alive, asks questions that make the reader uneasy and thoughtful. And he adds drama and humor and inspiration.

They are not to be read and put down. His writing won't let you. You will find yourself reading, and studying, and thinking on these things.

The new *Arkansas United Methodist* and its predecessors are fortunate that the Rev. Mr. Powell wants to share his convictions and beliefs in their pages. And now he is broadening his audience, with a collection of his lessons in this book. We look forward to a wider readership for him and to his continued contributions to our paper.

Georgia M. Daily
Editor
Arkansas United Methodist
1986

Shades Of Columbus

IT IS OFTEN SAID of Christopher Columbus that when he left Spain, he did not know exactly where he was going. When he set foot on the shores of America, he did not know where he was, and when he returned to Spain, he did not know exactly where he had been. Particularly in the early days of a new year and as we begin once again to reflect during this new Lenten season, as Christians continuing our own voyages to new experiences, it will be to our advantage to arrive at a perspective somewhat clearer than that of Columbus.

1. *Know where we are going.* For the mature Christian, this question should carry us considerably beyond the kind of topical resolutions usually proposed at the beginning of a new year: lose weight, save more money, stop smoking, spend more time with the family, learn one new thing each day, and so on. These are all noble undertakings and any of us would be the better for observing them, but they simply do not push the matter far enough. Do we have a larger plan for our lives, some attainable, realistic objectives that we are attempting to achieve? Or, are we like the little boy's father who sat leisurely whittling on the doorstep. When the little fellow asked, "What ya doing?" the father replied, "Nothing." The lad thought for a moment and then asked, "How will you know when you're finished?" The truth is, the man was simply "filling in time" by aimless whittling. Similarly, there are those persons who "whittle" away day after day with no personal objective in mind, no intentional effort, waiting instead to be blown about by whatever friendly breeze that blows. We are created to achieve, to know where we are going, and to do all for the glory of God. The Scriptures assure us that whatever we undertake under the leadership of the Spirit, God will baptize with his grace. Centuries ago, when an entire people took up an objective of mammoth proportions, the promise was

given, "When you pass through the waters I will be with you; and through the rivers, they shall not overwhelm you; when you walk through fire you shall not be burned, and the flame shall not consume you." (Isaiah 43:2) That promise was honored. Where are you going as a person? Where are we going as a church?

I was speaking once with a friend about accepting Christ into his life and becoming active in the church. The purpose of the church, he claimed, was ambiguous to him. "Exactly what is it the church is trying to accomplish?" he asked. How would you answer such a question?

2. *Know where we are.* Are we now at the point we had hoped to be? Are we closer to God now than we were last week, last year? Knowing where we are going is not always apparent. A man was sitting with his wife in a concert hall listening to the lady on stage sing one difficult selection after another. The man, bored and restless, leaned to the gentleman beside him and whispered, "She's not very good is she?" The gentleman replied, "I'll have you know she is my wife!" "Oh," the man stumbled, attempting to redeem himself, "I mean the music she is singing is not all that good is it?" The gentleman sighed, "I wrote the music." We do not always know where we are, but one thing is for certain, we are God's creation, set in some arena for service. No matter where we are, we are precious and loved. Isaiah 43:4 reads, "Because you are precious in my eyes, and honored, and I love you. . . ."

Dr. Gene Bartlett, a minister in the American Baptist Church, tells that one morning as he left the parsonage to walk to the church, one of his sons heard the door slam and suddenly remembered he had something to discuss with his father. Down the stair, through the house, out the front door, and down the street the boy ran yelling to his father. Dr. Bartlett says his son's face showed strain, anxiety, and fear that he would not reach his father. He did however, and the conversation took place. That afternoon Bartlett walked home and saw the boy playing in the yard. He called his son's name and the boy turned happily to run to him. This time, the boy's face showed security, assurance, and acceptance. The difference in the two encounters, Bartlett says, is that he first called the boy's name. In that moment, he learned the meaning of the phrase, "He has *first* loved us." No matter where we are, we are precious and *first* loved of God.

3. *Know where we have been.* It is important to know that wherever we have been, we have been in a state of grace. One of Israel's great recollections was its escape from Egypt. Grace had brought them up out of the land of the Pharaohs, provided quail and manna in the desert when there was nothing to eat, water from a rock when there was nothing to drink, and a fiery-cloudly pillar to guide them when they did not know which way to go. We have been in our own Egypts and, like the hymn-writer, we know that it is grace which "has brought us safe thus far, and grace will lead us home." God's grace is for "every one who is called by my name, whom I created for my glory, whom I formed and made." (43:7)

It is good to know where we have been, to know where we are, and where we are going.

As the Twig Is Bent

2 Timothy 3:14-17

JESUS SAT as a child with other Jewish children on the dirt floor of the synagogue in Nazareth to receive instruction from the rabbi. Paul studied at the feet of Gamaliel. John Wesley received instruction at his mother's knee and later received formal training from some of the most outstanding scholars of his time. Instruction served them, as it serves us, as a strong potion. We are not speaking of education in general here, though the same claim may be made for it. Some things can be learned on one's own and achieved from personal experience apart from instruction. The focus here is upon that part of our knowledge which has come to us through intentional instruction. There are simply some things which we must be told and have translated or explained.

We are impressed that Jesus was commonly referred to as "Teacher." With all due respect to the group-dynamics people, Jesus did not arrange his hearers in a circle, arm himself with magic markers and newsprint, and ask, "All right, what do you want to talk about today?" To be sure, that is a legitimate technique for group sharing which indeed maximizes general participation, but Jesus chose to *instruct*. There were some things he had to tell which his listeners did not always know to ask, and we marvel not only at what he told, but also at the never-to-be-forgotten manner in which he told it. His instruction gathered meaning from the ordinary: yeast, birds, lilies, foxes, lost coins, sheep, patches on garments, bridegrooms, vineyards, seed, and the like. Even a major instruction in the closing hours of his ministry, the Last Supper, involved two articles which he knew would be on every table as a daily reminder of the lesson: bread and wine.

The Psalmist too, was given to putting his material in a manner easily remembered. For example, Psalm 119 cleverly arranges its lesson in acrostic form. The 176 verses contain seventy-two stanzas. Each stanza begins with a sequential letter of the Hebrew alphabet until all twenty-two letters are used. Simply stated, anyone who could remember the alphabet could memorize the Psalm.

Instruction informs. Information annihilates ignorance. Someone has claimed that we live in a day when we are faced with "third generation Biblical illiterates." What a challenge to those of us who are called to instruct. Moreover, the popular quip, "You can believe anything and belong to such-and-such church" would seem to indicate that instruction is either not being laid out or is not being retained.

Instruction prepares. Alexander Pope put it simply: "Just as the twig is bent, the tree's inclined."

Instruction serves. Tools for, the journey and knowledge for the doing! Read 2 Timothy 3:14-17 and reflect on how religious instruction is profitable to those who aspire to follow the way of Christ. How is the Word of God, as the Psalmist proclaims, a "lamp to our feet and a light to our paths"?

THREE OBSERVATIONS about Isaiah's "Song of the Vineyard":

1. *It was a song.* That is to say, it was a marked variation in the prophet's manner of proclamation. Isaiah was an eloquent, forthright orator, not a balladeer. It has been suggested that the reason for this temporary departure in style may have been the circumstances at that particular time. Deuteronomy 16:13-16 describes the carnival-like atmosphere which occurred in the ancient Feast of Booths. Some commentators have surmised that Isaiah rendered this specific message at such an occasion, in a manner consistent with the mood of the observance. However, there was perhaps another reason for the message being contained in a song.

It has been told that Arkansas' own Jimmy Driftwood was once a teacher in the public school system. It seems that in the course of his instruction, he was given the unenviable responsibility of teaching American History to an especially rowdy, belligerent group of students who either misbehaved or daydreamed throughout his lectures. Driftwood, a singer and songwriter, decided to undertake an experiment. He set a portion of the history lesson to music and somehow managed to get his maverick charges to sing along with him. "In 1814 we took a little trip, we went with Colonel Jackson down the mighty Mississip." When the song was finished, the class remembered it, continued to sing it throughout the day and days following, and enjoyed having learned about the Battle of New Orleans in a way they could remember. Novel, yes, but the message was clearly conveyed and, just as importantly, *remembered.* Perhaps there is more significance to Isaiah's "Song of the Vineyard" than first meets the eye.

2. *The Song was a parable.* God had planted Israel as a vineyard on a high place. He anticipated a magnificent yield.

God had cleared the land of impediments to growth (Canaanites and others), planted premium vines, and set a watchtower over the vineyard. But alas, the harvest turned out to be sour fruit.

3. *The song was the basis for Jesus' Parable of the Vineyard.* Compare Isaiah's song of the vineyard with Mark 12:1-12. For both accounts, Jeremiah 2:21 provides a fitting epilogue: "I planted you a choice vine, wholly of pure seed. How then have you turned degenerate and become a wild vine?"

Living with the Consequences

Deuteronomy 30:17-18

I SUPPOSE it would have been a far easier, more convenient thing for God to have created robots instead of offspring capable of making choices. If Adam and Eve had not been cognizant, thinking individuals with the ability of choosing, the Garden of Eden would probably still be in full flower. If Absolom had been a puppet, history would surely remember him as something other than a long-haired renegade son. If Jonah had not had a choice, there would be no story of Jonah and the "great fish." If Christ had not had a choice, the Cross would be reduced to a foreordained act of brutal cosmic drama. If we had no choice, there would be no such thing as sin, for we could not responsibly do either good or bad. However, God loved humanity enough, trusted it enough, to bless it with choice. The blessing appears at times to be a curse. Even Paul lamented, "For the good that I would I do not; but the evil which I would not, that I do." (Romans 7:19)

None of us need to be reminded that our choices are accompanied by consequences. Sometimes the passing of time is required, but we inevitably get the message. Our greed for quick crops several decades ago resulted in overplanting. The consequence, as we know, was the Dust Bowl. Many manufacturers have chosen to have a greater regard for profits than for properly caring for the waste and pollution created by factories and plants. The consequence has been that our lungs and atmosphere, streams and wildlife are paying the price for that choice. Our military chose to broadcast "Agent Orange" (a toxic herbicide) over millions of acres in Vietnam as a defoliant during the war. The consequence was not only that vegetation was defoliated, but it is now believed to be responsible for deaths, genetic mutations, cancer, and other diseases among our own veterans. Americans continue to choose a lifestyle which requires far more than our share of world resources.

15

The consequence is poor stewardship on the one hand and resentment from other countries on the other.

God could have made it much easier on himself had he created robots, but he trusted us enough to give us a choice. The consequence is, we have made some bad choices.

In verse 15 of our text, the alternatives are set before Israel: "I have set before you this day life and good, death and evil." The consequence is told in verse 16: "If you obey the commandments of the Lord your God. . . by loving the Lord your God, by walking in his ways, and by keeping his commandments. . . then shall you live and multiply, and the Lord your God will bless you in the land."

Moses asked Israel to choose. The choice sounds familiar, as does the consequence.

The Gospel on Trial   Acts 21:10-14

LET US BEGIN by abruptly relating three contemporary examples:

1. In late March of 1981, a mother drove her son John to an airport in Denver, put him out, and told him not to come home again. He didn't. A few days after being dropped off at the airport, John Hinckley shot and wounded President Ronald Reagan, presidential press secretary James Brady, Secret Service agent Timothy McCarthy, and D. C. police officer Thomas Delahanty. A grim reminder that *we inhabit a violent society*.

2. Israel, the same family of earth from which emerged Jesus of Nazareth 2,000 years ago, today is the largest supplier of weapons to at least three countries in Central America. We live in *a world of contradictions*.

3. A recent ad in the *New York Times* invited persons to purchase a high-rise on Manhattan's swank east side, and drive away in a free 1983 Rolls-Royce Silver Spirit. Apartments range from $583,000 to $1.2 million, but the automobile is free. Meanwhile, unemployment cripples thousands of our fellow citizens, and people stand in line to receive surplus cheese. Our society extends from the *irresponsibly affluent to the painfully poor*.

Change the examples above, but retain the italicized phrases, and see how similar our world is to that of Paul's. The gospel was on trial then; it is on trial today. Has there been a time when it has not been on trial?

Both the Gospel and Paul were on trial in Jerusalem. But then again, as we have seen in Paul's letters, the apostle had actually been on trial in Macedonia, Thessalonica, Beroea,

17

Athens, Corinth, and Ephesus. Oh, he was not dragged into court in those places, but he was on trial all right. And now he had come to Jerusalem, bearing an offering collected from the Gentile churches. He had been warned not to enter the city (21:10-14), but he still came. Soon, he stood before Ananias, the Sadducees, and Pharisees . . . on trial again. Whether intentional or incidental, Paul managed to accomplish a ruse which worked to his advantage. He reminded the assembly that he was a Pharisee and that he had been brought before them with respect to the resurrection. The Sadducees did not believe in a resurrection, angels, or spirits; the Pharisees did. Shortly, they were so busy arguing among themselves that they forgot the real issue and Paul was dismissed.

Can you think of instances where Christians have been so busily engaged with arguing among ourselves that we have forgotten the real issue or reason for our existence?

Preparing for the Wrong Thing

ACCORDING TO JEWISH RELIGIOUS LAWS the eldest son of a family was entitled to inherit twice the share as the younger brother. (Deuteronomy 21:15-17) In all probability the person who approached Jesus in our text was a younger brother who wanted more than his legal share of an inheritance. Jesus replied to the subject at hand by citing the parable of the "Rich Young Fool." The bottom line of the parable is that the rich fool had prepared for the wrong thing. He had taken his goods into account, but had made up no provision for his own soul.

A dear couple in another city, exceptionally active in the church I was serving at the time, constructed a storm cellar in their back yard. Over a period of several months both of them had shoveled dirt, poured concrete, laid blocks, and literally built the cellar themselves. Soon after it was completed, they invited me out to see what they had accomplished. Understandably proud, they pointed out the neat, solid blockwork of the exterior and called attention to the more than adequate drain-offs. Inside, every provision was made in the event of an extended stay. It was an exceptional storm cellar in all respects, and in every sense of the word, they were more than prepared for a storm. However, in a few short weeks, both of them were killed by a speeding motorist as they attempted to turn from the highway into their driveway. Despite meticulous preparations, the fact remains that they had prepared for the wrong thing. But you say, "It is impossible to prepare for the unexpected!" Yes, that is precisely one of the points Jesus was attempting to underscore in our scriptures.

A young businessman, workaholic, full of hustle and drive, spends twelve hours each day at the office. His wife asks him to come home early to eat the evening meal with the family,

19

but no, he must chase the distant horizon. While other children's fathers take them to the park, his children find solace in video games. When the wife says he ought to spend more time with the children, he replies that he has given them everything they will ever need. When she complains about his hours, he reminds her of the diamonds she has on her fingers. He had prepared for their every need, right down to the insurance. One day he is summoned to the hospital to be by the bedside of his oldest daughter who has overdosed on drugs. Two days later, he has a heart attack and is told by the doctor that he must change his lifestyle drastically. He has not prepared for any of that.

Jesus asked the rich fool, "And the things you have prepared for, whose will they be?" Are we prepared to deal with that question?

Genes of Joash

THIS IS A DIFFICULT, and not-too-pretty story to tell. Let us begin by identifying some of the principle characters: Athaliah, daughter of Jezebel, married Jehoram the king of Judah. Like her mother, she was a fanatical champion of Baal worship. She was directly responsible for the desecration of the Jerusalem Temple, the conversion of its sacred vessels into articles used for Baal worship, inciting a general massacre, and seizing the royal throne which she occupied for six years. Ahaziah, son of Athaliah and father of Joash. Joash, who had been rescued as an infant from an attempt to exterminate the royal line by Jehoshabeath, who cared for him secretly for six years. Joash became king at age seven, served well until the death of Jehoiada, then came under the influence of the wicked princes of Judah. Jehoiada, a priest who had educated Joash and made a positive influence upon his character. Zechariah, a prophet and son of Jehoiada, whom Joash had killed for spreading the truth.

Some commentators suggest that Joash was the product of bad genes. There is a case for this claim insofar as his great-grandfather was King Ahab (who sponsored Baal worship), his great-grandmother was Jezebel, his grandfather King Jehoram, an evil king who "departed with no one's regret," (12:20) and his grandmother, Athaliah. Not a distinguished gallery of progenitors. Other commentators hold that Joash was the product of his environment, doing well under the influence of Jehoiada, but bottoming out while in the company of the princes of Judah. Both suggestions it appears to me, take the heat off Joash's own *choices,* placing the responsibility either on his genes or his environment. I submit that there have been too many individuals who have risen above either genes or environment to become noteworthy for either suggestion to be the "be all, end all." Mary McLoud Bethune, Charles Tindley, Booker T. Washington, Helen Keller, a multitude of historical achievers, as well as persons we know personally, take away Joash's alibi. The point is, at some significant time in our lives, we each decide at which level we choose to compete and express. Joash, despite whatever influence his genes and environment had upon him, *chose* the lowlife. At which level do we compete?

Unfulfilled Potential Judges 16:30

LET US REVIEW some of the exploits of Samson:

- In the vineyards of Timnah, he "tore a lion assunder . . . and he had nothing in his hand." (Judges 14:5-6)
- He went down to Ashkelon and killed thirty men because they had learned the answer to a riddle from his wife. (14:10-19)
- He caught three hundred foxes, knotted lighted fire-brands in their tails, and set them loose in the grain fields of the Philistines. (15:1-5)
- He was bound by the Philistines with two new ropes, but the Spirit of the Lord came upon him and released him. He then found "a fresh jawbone of an ass" and slew a thousand men. (15:9-17)
- He judged Israel in the days of the Philistines for a period of twenty years. (15:20)
- At midnight, he carried the doors of the Gaza City gates, two door posts, bars and all, to "the top of the hill that is before Hebron." (16:1-3)
- He was bound with seven fresh bowstrings but snapped them from his body as if they were paper. (16:8-9)
- He grasped the two middle pillars which supported the temple of Dagon, and removed them, causing the temple to fall, killing more than three thousand persons. (16:29-30)

To Samson, life was apparently one fun-filled, irresponsible frolic after another and, in a word, he tragically "wasted" himself. Delilah, the Philistines, his blindness, and his final feat of strength at the temple of Dagon were all actually footnotes to the larger theme of Samson's life; he forgot God and wasted himself.

There is suggestive evidence that Samson did not have the monopoly on frivolity and unfulfilled potential: 1. twenty-three million Americans, or one in five adults, lack reading skills and writing abilities to handle minimal demands of daily living; 2. an eighteen-year-old New Yorker named Ben dreads using the subway because he cannot read the names of stations; 3. a top eastern law firm has hired a professional writing instructor to work with newly graduated lawyers because many of them cannot write; 4. two-thirds of our colleges and universities find it necessary to provide remedial reading; 5. in a certain high school English class, eighty-eight percent of the students could not name the four Gospels. One boy said that three of them are named Christianity, Hinduism, and Confusion, but he did not know the name of the other one; 6. at the University of Denver, a student was asked on a test, "Tell what you know about Moses." He answered frankly, "All I know about Moses is that he is dead."

Samson did not have a monopoly on unfulfilled potential and the "wasted" life.

IT IS COMMONLY ACCEPTED that the first Church Council met in Jerusalem sometime between A.D. 44-47. Acts 15:4-19 relates that a major part of the agenda was concerned with the matter of whether or not circumcision should be required of Gentile converts. The Jerusalem party said "Yes", while Paul and Barnabas, who were not requiring circumcision of their new converts said "No." A lengthy debate ensued, followed by a brief statement by Peter: "And after there had been much debate, Peter rose and said to them, 'Brethren . . . why do you make a trial of God by putting a yoke upon the neck of the disciples which neither our fathers or we have been able to bear? But we believe that we shall be saved through the grace of the Lord Jesus Christ, just as they will.'" (10-11)

Peter's arugment against requiring circumcision of Gentile converts was followed by a pronounced silence within the assembly. After a while, Paul and Barnabas recounted some of the "signs and wonders" which God had accomplished through them among the Gentiles. Finally, James, the leader of the church in Jerusalem and, according to one tradition, the brother of Jesus, concluded the matter with an authoritative judgment: "Brethren . . . my judgment is that we should not trouble those of the Gentiles who turn to God" (13-19).

The Council has decided: 1. salvation hinges upon but one requirement — faith in Jesus Christ; 2. Christianity would widen it's orbit to become a world religion. The message of Christ was conceived to be too wonderful to be confined to a clique, territory, or any exclusive setting; 3. Christianity, unlike a religion based upon legalism, is a matter of the spirit.

The issue had clearly been what Charles M. Laymon calls the matter of "Christ-plus." "Christ-plus" refers to whether or not salvation requires anything in addition to faith in Christ. In other words, is salvation understood to mean faith in Christ *plus* something else? Unfortunately, it is not unusual to observe certain Christians who insist that salvation requires faith in Christ *plus* participation in a specific mode of baptism, or manner of observing the Lord's Supper, or actually belonging to a particular fellowship. Exclusiveness erects fences. Jesus Christ tears down fences.

John Bunyan in his immortal allegory, Pilgrims' Progress, told of the pilgrim who set out from the City of Destruction for the City of Life. Pilgrim will forever be known as a selfish and unworthy man because he made the pursuit of his own salvation his chief aim in life, leaving his own family behind in the City of Destruction. Devoted though he was, he was yet misled by the "Christ-plus" attitude.

Salvation is not so much a matter of what one must *do,* as a matter of what Christ has already *done* in our behalf.

Eternally Interceding

Eternally Interceding Exodus 32:1

THE HEBREW PEOPLE knew that Moses was on Mount Sinai, but it seemed to them that he had been gone much longer than necessary. All manner of mummerings arose within the ranks. Had he deserted them? Had something happened to him? Finally, it was decided that they would raise up Aaron as their new leader. Moreover, an idol fashioned in the form of a golden bull was set in their midst as the new object of worship. Unexpectedly, Moses returned. The scene which followed included at least three emphases:

1. *Pronouncement.* God utters a blistering assessment of the Hebrew people: "I have seen this people, and behold, it is a stiff-necked people." (32:9) Then follows an expression of his intention; "Now therefore let me alone, that my wrath may burn hot against them and I may consume them." (32:10) As the Revelator was to put it centuries later, Israel had "forgotten its first love." Even as Moses was on the mountain top receiving the Ten Commandments, the people were fawning around the golden idol which had been fashioned from their own jewelry. It had been remarked that the people were just out of slavery . . . they were tired of waiting on Moses to return to them . . . they wanted to celebrate somehow and thank somebody. Not yet understanding the character of Moses' God, they manufactured their own god to enable them to focus their celebration upon *something.* I believe the observation is correct inasmuch as we see latter-day versions of similar behavior, i.e., persons who want to celebrate life but are unable to understand the God of Christianity take unto themselves golden calves in some form or another. There are different causes of a stiff neck. Some are caused by sleeping in a draft, some are congenital, others due to injury or disease, and still others by arrogance and stubbornness. It is the latter malady to which God is referring in 32:9, the neck so stiff that it cannot bow

27

to God. At the time of God's pronouncement to Moses, the Hebrew people were in fact, in the words of Jonathan Edwards, "sinners in the hands of an angry God."

2. *Intercession.* Moses did not attempt to excuse his people, but instead undertook to intercede for them. He went to God in their behalf. I remember the story of the frail little country boy whose parents were so poor that they could not feed their family properly. The little boy , always undernourished, was sluggish and scarcely felt up to completing his assignments at school. One day the teacher announced the assignment and warned that anyone not completing it would be punished. Sure enough, the pale little youth failed to turn his work in when it was due. The teacher called him forward to the desk and told him to bend over. His hollow eyes looked helplessly at her as his bony body braced itself for a whipping. As he bent over, the bones in his back made little ridges in his shirt and his baggy pants were evidence of skinny legs and a tiny waist. The teacher raised the paddle. Suddenly, a little boy raised his hand and said, "Teacher, can I take his whipping for him?" That is a secular case of intercession. A theological case is "and while we were yet sinners, Christ died for us," and as the letter to the Hebrews suggests, Christ is "eternally interceding in our behalf."

3. *Mercy.* Certainly God was angry with the Hebrew people, just as he is vexed and saddened by those of us who become so stiff-necked that we cannot bow in an attitude of gratefulness for his leadership in our lives and the grace which always goes before us. It is often remarked, "When I stand before God in the judgment, I won't ask for justice, I will ask for mercy." To be sure, none of us could survive the justice, but because of God's promise to Moses, and the intercession of Christ, we do believe that there is *hope for the sinner* because a part of God's character is mercy.

A Matter of Excess   Mark 6:30-44

BEFORE COMMENTING directly about Mark 6:30-44, allow me to direct your attention to two Old Testament stories.

1. The first story is found in 2 Kings 4:1-7 and concerns the widow of a prophet whose creditors were about to foreclose her outstanding debt. Additionally, her two sons were to be carried away as slaves. Beside herself, the widow cried out to Elisha for help. Elisha asked her if she had anything in the house of value which might be sold to provide money toward the debt. "Only a partially filled jar of oil," she answered. Elisha surprisingly instructed her to go throughout the community collecting jars to be filled with her oil. We are probably safe to assume that if she did not feel rather foolish, there is a good chance her sons did. Here she went, gathering empty jars to hold the little bit of oil which did not nearly fill the jar it was in. When it was all said and done however, there was more oil than jars to put it in, enough money was available to pay the creditor, and the excess was sufficient for the widow and her boys to live on.

2. The other story is also found in 2 Kings and again deals with excess. A man brought Elisha twenty loaves of barley bread and was instructed by the prophet to feed a rather sizeable gathering. The man asked, "How can I feed 100 men with only twenty loaves of bread?" To make a long story short, let's read the conclusion of the account: "Then he set it before them and they ate and had some left over." (2 Kings 4:42-44)

The account in Mark 6:30-44 bears striking similarities to the incidents mentioned above, especially the latter. For this reason, the feeding of the 5,000 is understood by many to be Jesus' confirmation that his ministry was in the prophetic tradition of Elisha and under the authority of God. That is one way to interpret the miracle.

Another explanation was offered years ago by the distinguished Christian, Albert Schweitzer, who believed that the feeding of the 5,000 was an "eschatological sacrament" which was in fact a foretaste, or preview, of the greater feast to be held in the approaching Kingdom of God.

Of course, the simplest explanation is that Jesus was addressing a specific need at a specific time, and that that is the whole of it. However, let us not overlook the emphasis that Mark places upon the miracles of Christ as signs of his authority. We would perhaps be well within the mark to accept all three possibilities as legitimate.

I particularly like the quantity measure in the Elisha stories, the feeding of the 5,000 and other incidents throughout the Scriptures. The provisions were not merely sufficient for the immediate need, but always resulted in *excess*. Surely that must suggest something to us of the mind of God. His grace and love are more than sufficient for our needs.

Daring Words

THE GOSPEL ACCORDING TO MARK, commonly accepted to be the earliest of the synoptics, relates that Jesus began his Galilean ministry by 1. making an announcement, 2. extending an invitation, and 3. issuing a command. It would be pressing the matter entirely too far to even remotely suggest that the sequence of events was intentional, yet there is a certain familiarity about the sequence itself. As a matter of fact, the three ingredients, broadly categorized above, probably bear a striking resemblance to the sermon you will likely hear in your particular church on any given Sunday: a. the announcement of a Gospel truth; b. the exhortation, with some degree of urgency, to accomplish something in the name of Christ, and c. the invitation to respond. Intentional or not, Jesus began his ministry with a format exceptionally accommodating to Gospel preachers. However, let us take up the sequence as described by Mark.

1. *The announcement.* The arrest of John the baptizer apparently served as the catalyst for Jesus to reveal the messianic secret. For thirty years, he had maintained a low profile, preparing himself, shaping his perspectives, waiting — waiting for the proper time to thrust himself prominently into the midst of human affairs. At last, the moment had arrived: "The time is fulfilled, and the kingdom of God is at hand; repent, and believe in the gospel." (1:15) Daring words! He had made bold as a young man sometime earlier in his hometown synagogue to proclaim that the Scriptures had been fulfilled at his reading. The Nazarenes responded by chasing him from the community. He knew full well that there would be a more general uprising against him now by both civil and religious authorities. But there was no choice. The groundwork had been laid, preparations had been completed, John was in prison, and the alarm must continue to be sounded: "The kingdom of God is at hand; repent, and believe in the gospel."

2. *The invitation.* He would need help. Passing along the Sea of Galilee he saw two brothers, Simon and Andrew. Without the slightest qualification, he said to them, "Follow me and I will make you fishers of men." Take notice that no questions were asked, no excuses offered, no "process planning" nor introspective "objective-setting" dialogue transpired. Mark says, "And immediately they left their nets and followed him." Going a little farther, two other brothers, James and John heard a similar, abrupt invitation to respond in like manner. How do you account for the fact that these four individuals, secure in employment, having obligations and immediate responsibilities, walked away from it all to follow one who had come upon them from behind, no questions asked? Perhaps a part of the answer is found in 1:22 where Jesus is referred to as one who spoke with "authority," and not as the scribes. This particular reflection upon the scribes, implying a certain insipidness, interests us. They possessed authority by virtue of their position. Why did they not speak with authority? Conjecture is risky business, but we have a notion that their recitations were mechanical, unfeeling, and sing-song. Devotion may have been reduced to formalized vocation, and the sharp edge of adeptness dulled by neglect. Figureheads occupy space but command little respect, whether they be scribes, ministers, bishops, church-school teachers, or members of a church staff. One must be more than simply a "figure-head." Perhaps we should each take counsel with ourselves regarding the phrase, "for he taught as one having authority, not as the scribes."

3. *The command.* Jesus rebuked an unclean spirit and commanded it to come out of a man in the synagogue, "and the unclean spirit . . . came out of him." (1:26) Let us note the response: "They were all amazed and said 'With authority he commands even the unclean spirits.' " (1:27)

Jesus began his public ministry with an *announcement,* an *invitation,* and a *command,* but most of all with *authority.*

Eyes on the Unseen

THE FIRST SCRIPTURE SELECTION relates the healing of a man "who was deaf and had an impediment in his speech." Although nothing is mentioned regarding the faith of the man who was healed, faith was yet an active ingredient in the healing as exhibited by those who resolutely brought the man to Jesus. In verse 34, the phrase "looking up to heaven," underscores the intimate relationship with God that Jesus brought to that moment. Similarly, I have read that when Francis of Assisi preached, he never looked at his hearers, but instead fixed his eyes upon the sky as if expecting Christ to appear before he had completed the next sentence. Jesus, "looking up to heaven," apparently sought to acknowledge and intensify the power of God in his life for this moment of healing.

In our second passage, faith again is important to the healing, but this time it is the faith of the person to be healed, Bartimaeus. By faith, Bartimaeus cried out to Jesus even after being rebuked by those around him: "but he cried out all the more, Son of David, have mercy on me." (v.48) Although blind, he threw off his cloak and ran to where Jesus was standing. Jesus said, "What do you want me to do for you?" and by faith Bartimaeus replied, "Master, let me receive my sight." (v. 51) Jesus' reply underscores the point; "Go your way; your FAITH has made you well." (v. 52)

A congregation I once served included a young man who had been deaf from birth. He was a big, robust, handsome fellow whose sweet spirit enabled him to smile easily. During worship, he stood for the hymns and responsive readings, and participated as best he could in the entire service. During the sermon, his eyes were steadily fixed upon my lips, and in those few times when he was unable to lip-read what I was saying, he would turn to the young lady beside him and "sign" for clarification. I remember the day that he and the young lady came to my study to make plans for their wedding. She asked such questions as necessary and signed to him at intervals. As I spoke, she continued to interpret, even though he seemed already to understand. During the wedding ceremony, they held written copies of the vows and signed their pledges to each other. Before I left that congregation to acccept another appointment, the young man underwent an operation which enabled him to hear his first sounds. That was the first step. By God's grace, one day, perhaps even now, he will be able to listen to all those things which you and I have grown accustomed to. Although different than the deaf man who was brought to Jesus, it *will* be a genuine miracle of healing, and it will have been done for one who has cried out from the silence in *faith*.

We are far removed in time and space from ancient Jericho where our Scriptures relate two of our Lord's healings. However, as a society and as individuals, we yet stand in need of the healing touch.

Charles H. Scott's familiar hymn says it well; "Open my eyes that I may see, glimpses of truth Thou hast for me . . . Open my ears that I may hear voices of truth Thou sendest clear." And then the all-important third verse concludes, "Open my mouth and let me bear gladly the warm truth everywhere."

Faith and Expectation

ACTS 1:4-14 contains certain encouragements to the followers of Christ to be an "expectant" fellowship. With this in mind, let us consider some specific instances where expectancy is implied.

1. Acts 1:5: "For John baptized with water but before many days you shall be baptized with the Holy Spirit." What is the difference between John's water baptism and the baptism of the Holy Spirit?

   a. *John's baptism.* Water baptism was commonly practiced by the Jews long before the appearance of John. It symbolized religious purification, and in a more specialized use it was applied when new converts entered into Judaism (proselyte baptism). John, however, baptized both Jews and Gentiles as a rote of moral purification for the approaching Kingdom of God. Although John's baptism would enable those who submitted to it to meet the "Day of the Lord," it was to be distinguished as different from a future baptism, administered by one who "will baptize you with the Holy Spirit and fire."

   b. *Baptism of the Holy Spirit.* This baptism consists not in symbolic gestures of initiation, but in the receiving of "power." It does not ordain anybody for, or against, the future but rather manifests itself in a spiritual experience in the present. An initiatory baptism is symbolically accomplished *once*, whereas the baptism of the Holy Spirit may occur quite unrehearsed many times over. The element of *expectation* is contained in the selected scripture by the phrase, "But before many days, you shall be baptized with the Holy Spirit."

2. Acts 1:7-8: "It is not for you to know times or seasons

which the Father had fixed by his own authority. But you shall receive power when the Holy Spirit has come upon you." The disciples have just asked Jesus a legitimate question regarding the nature of his mission. A simple "yes" or "no" answer would not have been sufficient inasmuch as if he replied, "Yes (I have come to restore the Kingdom of Israel)," it would have been a lie, and if he had replied "No," they would have become disillusioned with him in the beginning. Instead, he informs them that it is not for them to know all the mysteries of God — but there is a consolation: "You shall receive power when the Holy Spirit has come upon you." Perhaps it is like saying to someone, "You cannot adequately define love, but nonetheless you can experience it." Here, the power of the Holy Spirit is promised, and they are encouraged to *expect* it in their own experience.

3. Acts 1:11: "Men of Galilee, why do you stand looking into heaven?" I suppose the most logical answer would have been, "Because we are bewildered!" It would have been extremely difficult to have acted otherwise while witnessing their Lord being lifted up into heaven on a cloud. If that were not enough, two men in white robes suddenly appeared to stand by them and question their amazement. In all probability, at least one of the inferences here is that rather than gazing into heaven, it would be more proper to get on with the business of the Kingdom, teaching and preaching, and doing "whatsoever I have commanded you." However, they should pursue their tasks of soul-winning with an attitude of *expectancy* because "this Jesus, who was taken up from you into heaven, will come in the same way."

4. Acts 1:14. "All those with one accord devoted themselves to prayer." And we may be sure that their prayers contained *expectancy*. Expectancy for what? For the baptism of the Holy Spirit and the return of the risen Lord.

Faith and Power

MARK 4:37-41 is one of the many passages in the Bible which has been set to music. "Master, the tempest is raging! The billows are tossing high! The sky is o'er shadowed with blackness . . ." You recognize it. From childhood, we have sung the words to "Peace Be Still" and have loved to lift the refrain which concludes, "they all shall sweetly obey thy will . . ." Two primary elements are underscored in both the scripture and the hymn: the *power* of Christ and *faith* in Christ.

The Gospel according to Mark characterizes the ministry of Jesus as being a succession of "mighty works," indicative of his Sonship. Actually, the stilling of the storm is only the beginning of a series of incidents portraying the power of Christ. After the storm experience on the Sea of Galilee, Jesus and the disciples came to the other side of the sea into the country of the Gerasenes. Here they encountered a man who lived among the tombs, crying out in travail both day and night, inflicting injury upon himself and striking fear into the hearts of all who chance to see him. Frequently, he had been subdued and bound with chains, but such was his deranged agony that he tore away the fetters and ran about the tombs as a wild man. In a great display of power, Jesus freed the man from his torment (5:13) and "all marveled. Then, crossing to the other side of the sea, Jesus encountered a certain Jarius, a ruler of the synagogue, who prevailed upon him to accompany him to his home and heal his daughter." (5:23) On the way to the home of Jarius Jesus was "touched" by a desperate woman who had hemorraged for twelve years and, according to Mark 5:29, so great was the power of Jesus that the woman was immediately healed simply by touching his clothing. Not to be minimized here is Jesus' statement to the woman; "Daughter, your faith has made you well; go in peace and be healed from your disease." (5:34) Now the word comes that during the interval, Jarius' daughter has died. Reassuring

Jarius, Jesus said, "Do not fear, only believe." Approaching the house Jesus observed a gathering of people loudly mourning the death of the girl. Everyone was asked to wait outside the house save the little girl's parents and the disciples who had been selected to accompany Jesus to the house, Peter, James, and John. "Taking her by the hand, he said to her, 'Talitha cumi' which means 'Little girl, I say to you, arise.' And immediately the girl got up and walked." (5:41-42)

Power! That is the theme of Mark's section dealing with three successive miracles of Jesus. Read again the refrain of "Peace, Be Still" and see how it applied to each of the three incidents. See also the summons for faith. The disciples were scolded for their lack of faith, the woman with the issue of blood was rewarded because of her faith, and Jarius was encouraged to intensify the faith he already had exhibited by falling at the feet of Jesus. Desperation characterizes all three encounters, and all three contain the enacted teaching that the power of Christ is but half of the whole; the other half, which taps this power, is *faith*. Ironically, it would appear that we, too, learn the lesson best in times of desperation.

Hymns at Midnight

PAUL AND SILAS had been thrown into prison at Philippi because Paul had cast a demon from a slave girl. However, there were extenuating circumstances. It seems the slave girl allegedly had powers of divination which enabled her to engage in "fortune telling." Her owners had managed to turn her condition into a rather lucrative business. And, of course, when Paul removed the demon, he also eliminated the owner's profit. Let's think about that for a moment. Isn't it fortunate that some people cannot receive the joy of a blessing because of a bitter spirit? A young girl, who is described by commentators as being mentally deranged, is healed! And yet all her owners could think about was the money her healing was going to cost them. I am reminded of the woman who went into the hospital for a physical examination without the knowledge of the minister or anyone else in the church. When her tests confirmed that she was in excellent health, she was dismissed to go home. A few days later, when the minister learned she had been in the hospital, he stopped by to see her. She proceeded to scold him because neither he nor anyone at the church had been to see her in the hospital (one and one-half days). She was sadly unable to enjoy the good news about her health because she had a bitterness in her spirit. It was the same kind of attitude that put Paul and Silas in prison.

Paul and Silas were singing hymns in the cell and, about midnight, there was a great earthquake. The foundations of the jail quivered and shook. The doors were flung open and the fetters of all the prisoners were unfastened. When the jailer saw that the doors were opened he supposed the prisoners had escaped. Knowing that he would be held accountable, he drew his sword and was about to take his own life when Paul said, "Do not harm yourself, for we are all here." (v. 28) The jailer immediately fell to his knees before Paul and said, "What must I do to be saved?" Paul answered, "Believe in the Lord

Jesus Christ, and you will be saved." The jailer and his entire family were baptized and received into the fellowship of Christ. His life had been saved twice; once during the earthquake, and once from his own hand. Now he was saved for all eternity.

In all probability, the hymns which Paul and Silas were singing at midnight had little if anything to do with the Philippian jailer's conversion. I would suspect that the eartquake stood him mentally erect, causing him to get in touch with the condition of his spirit. An earthquake can do that. So can foxholes, tornadoes, or a doctor saying to us, "I'm afraid I have some bad news." These and similar situations which you could name confront us with reality in a hurry. The earthquake made its impact on the jailer.

However, the fact that Paul and Silas did not attempt to escape from their cell also impacted the jailer. The coincidences were too numerous to ignore; the hymn singing, the earthquake, the cell being opened, the fetters on all the prisoners unfastened, and . . . not the slightest attempt to escape. Something was going on here! The accumulation of events brought the jailer to his moment of conversion.

Let the record show that conversion may occur suddenly, in the twinkling of an eye, or it may come upon us slowly, cumulatively, as the result of assorted experiences and reflections. And in the simple story of the Philippian jailer, we find the format for conversion in its simplest form (16:29-31), regardless of time, place, or manner.

Man Up A Tree

EVERY CHURCH SCHOOL CHILD knows the story of Zacchaeus: "Zacchaeus was a wee little man, a wee little man was he; he climbed up in a sycamore tree, for Jesus he would see." For our purposes here, let us divide the story into three parts:

1. *The person.* Jericho was the gate city for Judea's trade with the East, which meant that it was also the checkpoint for customs on imports and exports. Zacchaeus, as "chief tax collector," was in charge of collections and overseer of all other tax collectors in his district. Consequently, he was not only entitled to whatever revenues he could manage for himself, but also a share of what had been taken in by the other collectors. Opportunities for self-enrichment abounded and, from all indications, Zacchaeus allowed none to escape him. I would expect that at a very early age it had become clear to him that his choices would be severely limited. He was not physically suited for life in the country, nor strong enough to be a merchant who must travel long distances to trade. His childhood peers doubtless reminded him of his size by numerous remarks and omissions. But there was apparently one thing he could do well: cipher. He would excel in the area of his strongest ability and greatest interest . . . money. The Scriptures depict him as short in stature, crooked in dealings, self-seeking, but interestingly enough, retaining a glimmer of moral consciousness.

2. *The encounter.* A large crowd had gathered to see Jesus as he passed through the city. Too small to see over the shoulders of others and unable to force his way to the front line, Zacchaeus climbed into a sycamore tree in order to see and, who knows, perhaps even to be seen. There is the possibility that the time had come in the little man's life when his spirit cried out for peace and security . . . the kind which the world cannot give . . . something he had been unable to achieve by a

lifetime of jaded aggressiveness. There is at least the possibility that something more than curiosity caused him to position himself in such a prominent place along the path of the one who was said to "forgive sinners." Whatever his reason, Jesus addressed him personally, went home with him to spend the day, and caused the people to complain, "He has gone in to be the guest of a man who is a sinner." (19:7)

3. *The transformation.* At some point during their visit, Zacchaeus stood up and said, "Behold, Lord, the half of my goods I give to the poor; and if I have defrauded anyone of anything, I will restore it fourfold." And Jesus said to him, "Today salvation has come to this house." (19:8-9)

The story of Zacchaeus is not an isolated incident. Other similarly tainted individuals have discovered that the deep places of their lives have been touched and embraced by one whose perception and discerning compassion penetrates beneath life's surface and addresses a lingering need. Had our Lord considered the tax collector as others saw him . . . niggardly, self-motivated, crooked, irritatingly ambitious . . . had our Lord stopped there, considering only the topical evidence, Zacchaeus would have been left up in the tree. But Jesus did not take his meal in the home of a reprobate that day; he supped with a man who had a *need*, and as the shadows of evening gathered about Jericho, the need of at least one of its citizens had been met; "Today salvation has come to this house."

A Maverick Son   2 Samuel 15:13-14

ABSALOM WAS BORN in Hebron. His first recorded experience is the pathetic story of the rape of his sister, Tamar. Later, during a feast he masterminded the slaying of Amnon after which he escaped to the home of his grandfather at Geshur where he remained for three years. Absalom approached Joab to intercede for him with David in an effort to be reinstated in the royal family. Joab refused twice. Absalom then proceeded to set fire to Joab's barley fields, forcing him to appear before David in order to escape the wrath of Absalom. In time, Absalom set about to undermine the people's confidence in David by exaggerating the evils of the king's court and presenting himself as the champion of the people. At the end of four years, confidence in David was sufficiently weakened and Absalom made bold to announce that at an appointed hour he would overthrow the throne of his father by force. David had no other recourse but to flee from Jerusalem. Eventually, the forces of father and son were to come up against each other in the forest of Ephraim, and the seasoned troops of David, under the leadership of Joab, Abishai, and Ittai the Hittite, utterly routed the forces of Absalom. As Absalom fled the battle upon his mule, his long hair became entangled in the thick branches of an oak tree, leaving him dangling helplessly in mid-air. Joab discovered him and slew him forthwith. Upon hearing the news, David cried out in one of the most pitiful laments in all the Scriptures: "O my son Absalom, my son Absalom! Would that I had died instead of you, O Absalom, my son, my son!" (2 Samuel 18:33)

There is a love which transcends all circumstances. It is not always within the scope of human rationality. The love of a parent for a child is a supreme reflection of such love. A parent may repeatedly scold a child for being irresponsible, lazy, undependable, and belligerent, but pity the poor person who dares to point out that child's shortcomings in front of that

43

child's parents. Love does not always operate within the limits of rationality.

The tragic story of David and his maverick son is favorably compared to the Gospel in miniature. In it are shades of Adam's folly, Israel's rebellion against God, the Prodigal Son, and many other instances of flagrant misconduct. But in them all, the Bible's theme of transcending love emerges most clearly. Not even the murder of God's own son could violate the most profound, powerful force in all the universe — love. God, like David, grieves because of love. It was Luther who remarked, "If I was God and the world treated me the way it treats God, I would dash the wretched thing to pieces." A rational conclusion. However, there is a love which operates beyond rationality and we are thankful to God for it.

A Steadfast Love Psalm 103

I RECENTLY was in the company of a minister friend who, between conversations, periodically hummed the tune to Charles Tindley's great old hymn, "Stand By Me." He frequently interrupted his humming to sing such verses as he could recall. In time, I inquired as to his fascination with that particular hymn. "Oh," said he, "we sang it in church this past Sunday and I've had it on my mind ever since. Besides, its always been one of my favorites."

We all have favorite hymns which impress themselves upon our lives until we find ourselves even unconsciously drawing upon their influence, don't we? Sometimes we are attracted first by the tune . . . at other times, the words . . . or at other times by the story of how the song came into being. We may be assured that the Psalms, the hymnbook of the Jewish people, contain many such songs which were hummed or sung aloud in the course of an ordinary day because they had become so indelibly imprinted upon the souls of a people who were able to "Sing the Lord's song (even) in a strange land." Psalm 103 is such a song. What a magnificent affirmation of faith! "Bless the Lord," it proclaims, and forget not the benefits of the One who forgives your iniquity, heals your diseases, redeems your life from the Pit, crowns you with *steadfast love* and mercy, and renews your youth like the eagles.

There is more here than a song. It is the verbalization of an experience. The Psalmist expressed the experience through music, the prophets through prophecy, Christ through Calvary, Paul through his life and letters, and multitudes of saints across the ages through their witness. God crowns us with *steadfast love!*

In 1874 Dwight L. Moody and Ira Sankey boarded a train in Glasgow, Scotland on their way to Edinburgh where Moody was to preach and Sankey was to lead the singing. Sankey perused a newspaper while Moody tended to some correspondence and jotted down notes for his sermon. Sankey was about to discard the newspaper when he noticed a little poem appearing in the corner of one of the pages. It had been written by a little orphaned Scottish girl who had died five years before the Glasgow paper had printed it as a "filler." Her name was Elizabeth Clephane. Sankey tore the poem from the paper and put it in his pocket with the thought of perhaps setting it to music one day. Later that evening in Edinburgh, Moody preached a sermon on "The Good Shepherd," then called on Sankey for a solo. Not having been told beforehand the subject of Moody's sermon, and certainly unprepared to sing, Sankey was taken by complete surprise. He had absolutely no idea what piece of music would be appropriate for the moment, even if he had had time to think about it. At a loss, he approached the pulpit, bowed his head for a moment, removed the little poem from his pocket. Without the slightest idea of a tune, he prayed for the Holy Spirit to direct him as he attempted to sing a poem which had no music. He began, "There were ninety and nine that safely lay in the shelter of the fold . . . ."

There is more than a song here. It is yet another verbalization of God's *steadfast love*.

The Power to Heal Mark 1:41-44

VERSE 41: "And Jesus, moved with compassion, put forth his hand, and touched him . . ." Apparently, compassion was not something ordinarily associated with religious exercise. The Sadducees practiced a highly formalized, impersonal, and legal program of religious discipline. The Pharisees were, in fact, "lay lawyers," whose self-righteousness and radical pursuit of the Law removed them from the common stream of humanity and established a separate pious caste. The Scribes were the experts in the interpretation and application of the Law, characterized more for brilliance than feeling. It is not surprising that people were able to distinguish Jesus immediately by his demeanor and manner. Unlike the experts, he "cared." The authority in his voice contained something more than knowledge and scriptural expertise, noticeably different than the scribes. "And they were astonished at his teaching, for he taught them as one who had authority, and not as the scribes." (1:22) Compassion was simply not in the experience of the religious professionals, and to actually come into bodily contact with an "unclean" person was unthinkable. However, verse 41 presents a marked contrast: "And Jesus, moved with compassion, put forth his hand, and touched him"

Verse 44a: "See that you say nothing to anyone." Let's go back for a moment to the experience in the New Testament referred to as "The Temptation." One of the requests made of Jesus was to throw himself from the pinnacle of the Temple and engage his supernatural powers to escape bodily injury. As had frequently been pointed out by numerous sources, this was an open invitation to Jesus to show his credentials as a "miracle worker," thus insuring a fast, enthuiastic following. However, it was not the intention of Jesus to gain notoriety on the strength of miraculous deeds. There was more to his ministry than miracles and he did not wish them to obscure his larger purpose. Just as he had resolved at the

47

temptation not to build his ministry around miracles, he discouraged the leper from heralding the cure he had received: ". . . Say nothing," or perhaps even, "Don't go running about telling everybody about my performing a miracle, or they may misinterpret my intentions."

Verse 44b: "Show yourself to the priest, and offer for your cleansing those things which Moses commanded, for a testimony to them." You may wish to turn to Leviticus 14 to read the specific type of offering a leper was to make. If the priests were convinced of his healing, a certificate would be issued to that effect which would, for all purposes, reinstate the bearer to community life. However, Jesus' purpose was to accomplish the healing in accordance with religious rite and legal custom, and continue to direct the man's thoughts toward praising God for cleansing.

Let us be careful not to overlook the cooperative element in the story; the leper provided the faith sufficient for such a miracle (v. 41), and Jesus provided the power.

Clean and Unclean

SIMON PETER is called into account by the Jewish Christians in Jerusalem to explain why he had made so bold as to eat unclean food in the presence of Gentiles. He explains that while he was in Joppa, a guest in the home of Simon the tanner, he had fallen into a trance and experienced a vision. Before going further, let us make a distinction at two points: 1. *Simon the tanner.* As the name suggests, Simon tanned hides, an occupation considered by Jews to be unclean, insofar as it involved handling dead things. (Leviticus 11:39-40), 2. *The vision.* While on the rooftop of Simon's house (11:5) Peter saw a great sheet being let down from heaven containing animals, beasts of prey, and wild birds. A voice instructed him to "rise, kill and eat," but refusing, he said, "No Lord, for nothing common or unclean has ever entered my mouth." But the voice answered, "What God has cleansed you must not call common." (11:9) Notice that Peter did not refer to the food as 'unclean,' but common, meaning 'beneath him.' Notice also that Peter is mildy chastized for placing himself above anyone or anything. The supreme point of the vision is found in 10:34: "Truly I perceive that God shows no partiality." It follows then, that if God's love is inclusive, "to the Gentiles also God has granted repentance unto life." (11:18) Yes, even the Gentiles, those who were outside the concern of the circumcision party in Jesusalem.

Closer to home, what about those who are outside the circle of our concern? Oh, we know about them well enough, but they are not a part of our daily experience, nor are they included in the regular routine of our decision-making. Occasionally, they may receive a polite tip of the hat, but they are included in the host of concerns outside our own family or church circle of concern which we are inclined to consider "unclean" or "common," reluctant to believe that even unto them also "God has granted repentance unto life." One at a time,

49

think about the following: Shall God grant repentance to 1. those in our prisons, 2. Russians, 3. criminals, 4. non-Christians, or even non-Christian religions, 5. persons who exploit us in some manner, 6. ignorant people who could do better but won't, 7. con-artists? Measure your response well, remembering that it was necessary for Peter to broaden the orbit of his concern.

A retiring old usher, instructing a youthful new replacement in the details of ushering said, "And remember, my boy, we have nothing but good, kind Christians in this church . . . until you try to put someone else in their pew." Perhaps the arena for extending the circle of our concern is nearer than we may suppose.

Tearing the Roof Off   Mark 2:1-5

IT SEEMS the scribes were always around. In our scripture we learn that Jesus was at his home in Capernaum. When word spread throughout the community, a great crowd gathered inside and out the house, prevailing upon Jesus to teach them. We are told that some of the scribes "were sitting there questioning in their hearts." Why were they there anyway? Out of curiosity? To heckle? To find fault? Were they acquaintances of Jesus that they could come into his home and find a place to sit while so many others were standing? I don't know . . . but it seems the Scriptures always bear the same foreboding comment, "the scribes were sitting there," or "nearby." At any rate, on this particular occasion, they got their eyes full.

First, there was a commotion. Four men were literally dismantling the roof of the house. When a large enough opening had been torn away, down came a pallet with a man on it. Although the Scriptures do not mention the scribe's reaction to the paralytic's rather crude entrance, we can imagine the sudden changing of their sophisticated expressions as they tugged nervously at their robes and mumbled beneath their breath. However, they may not have been surprised at all . . . they had joked among themselves that the Nazarene's clientele included harlots, tax collectors, the sick, unstable, ne'er-do-wells, and common sinners. Perhaps such an abrupt intrusion through the roof did not impress them at all, but was rather consistent with the kind of people attracted by the unorthodox carpenter. But again, that was but the beginning.

Jesus made bold to forgive the paralytic's sins! The scribes could sit still no longer: "Who can forgive sins but God alone?" Jesus replied, "Why do you question me like this? Let me ask you a question; which is easier to say to a paralytic, 'Your sins are forgiven,' or 'Rise, take up your pallet and walk?'" In a word, it is a small matter to mouth the words, 'Your sins are forgiven.' It *is* true that anyone can repeat these words whether they have the authority or not but in order that the scribes might know that Jesus possessed the authority, he did something more. Turning to the paralytic, he said, "Rise, take up your pallet and go home." To their astonishment, the paralytic did just that. He had received a double portion inasmuch as his sins had been forgiven and he had been physically healed. Additionally, the scribes had something to think about.

I want to say a word about the persistent souls who tore the roof off the house. Their determination is to be admired. Have you ever entertained the thought of visiting a sick friend or shut-in but decided against it because the weather was threatening, or the temperature was uncomfortable, or you were tired? Even the best of intentions are sometimes easily discouraged. Here were four men who could have turned away from the house when they saw such a crowd, thinking "we'll come again later." But no, they pushed their way through the crowd with the paralytic, climbed to the roof and made up their minds to get inside. They loved their friend enough to go to some extra effort, and they had absolute faith that the man inside could heal him. I hope I have a few friends like that. The paralytic owed a great deal of his recovery to his friends. What a combination: loving friends, persistent faith, and the touch of Christ!

WEBSTER'S DICTIONARY refers to "witness" in such terms as "testimony . . . to act as a witness of . . . to give or be evidence of." It is understandable that Jesus would use such metaphors as *salt* and *light* when speaking of the Christian witness

Salt. Salt was a valuable commodity in the ancient world, not uncommonly used as a bartering agent. As insignificant as the reference itself may seem, Jesus was actually dignifying the Church by referring to it in the sense of something rare and precious.

You are familiar with the expression, "That should be taken with a grain of salt." Sometimes things are said to us which are bland, tasteless, or even worse, in bad taste. Salt adds flavor which causes many items which we consume to become more palatable. The remark, "taken with a grain of salt" implies that some tasteless or crude remarks would go down better with a grain of salt. Salt adds flavor or zest. When Jesus commented, "You are the salt of the earth," he was implying that the Christian witness causes even the unfortunate, tasteless things in life to be more palatable. To remove the salt is to remove a prime ingredient to the whole of life itself, leaving it to the crude, base, and tasteless elements to prevail.

Matthew 5:13 continues, "But if salt has lost its taste, how shall its saltness be restored? It is no longer good for anything except to be thrown out and trodden under foot by men." Moffett translates the phrase more precisely: "If salt becomes insipid, what can make it salt again?" Insipid is the word. An insipid person is one who stands for nothing, contributes nothing, is dull, unimaginative, shallow, harmless, and a fence-straddler. Jesus encouraged the Church to be *salt*, avoiding insipidness.

Light. "You are the light of the world" is another familiar reference made in regard to the Christian witness. Indeed, a person does not light a lamp only to put it beneath a bushel where it cannot be seen. It is told that a congregation constructed a new sanctuary in which to worship. It was beautifully constructed, traditionally consistent with symbolic Christian architecture, practical in every consideration and lovely in every detail. Only one thing was omitted. There were no lights. Instead, little niches had been fashioned into the walls and window bases which were to hold candles. Each member was assigned a niche and told that he was to provide the candle for that particular spot. Otherwise, the spot would remain dark. In a very real sense, *they* were the light, and they got the message. They also understood that they were not only the light of the Church, but the "light of the world."

You and I are challenged to be the salt of the earth and the light of the world. The antithesis of the Christian witness is insipidness and darkness.

Creatures of Worth

GOD not only created persons, but persons of "worth."
Regrettably, the Genesis account of humanity's beginning has
frequently been sensationalized, either by recurring debates as
to the nature of the literature or gnat-straining arguments over
sequences, that the matter of "worth" has escaped the hearing of a people who desperately need to hear it. Whatever else
the high occurence of suicide in this country suggests to us,
the matters of low self-esteem and a consciousness of worth-
lessness must certainly be taken into account. Genesis is but
the first affirmation that God not only created persons, but
persons of *worth*.

In Matthew 6:26, Jesus said, "Look at the birds of the air:
they neither sow or reaped or gather in barns, and yet your
heavenly Father feeds them. Are you not of more value than
they?" Although his primary intent was to direct his hearers
beyond an anxiety-ridden life, the affirmation of worth is again
underscored. "Are you not worth more than they?" The in-
ference is "Yes," but how much more and why?

Years ago a little publication called *The Electric Ex-
perimenter* calculated what the average person weighing 150
pounds was worth. When the raw components were considered,
it was determined that the average person was composed of
3,500 feet of oxygen, nitrogen, and hydrogen; enough fats to
make a candle weighing fifteen pounds; enough carbon to make
9,360 lead pencils; fifty-four ounces of phosphorus to make
800,000 matches; enough sugar to make six little sugar cubes;
enough iron to make a ten-penny nail; enough lime to mark
off the batter's box on a baseball diamond; twenty spoonfulls
of salt; and various other chemicals and water which collec-
tively totaled $8.50. In consideration of current inflationary
costs, this means that a 150 pound person is presently valued
at almost fifteen dollars. Jesus said, "Are you not worth more
than they?" How much? From time to time it is remarked that

"so-and-so is worth a million dollars," or a certain athlete is worth twelve million. This is not the kind of worth we are concerned with here.

The Bible tells us that each child of God is a creature of unutterable worth. 1. We were created, not a little lower than the angels, but 'a little less than God.' Such a birthright overwhelms us with magnificent humility even as it elevates us to an honored estate; 2. 'For God so loved the world that he gave his only begotten Son . . .' We are worthy of the Son of God dying for us! What higher value can be placed on anything in the entire universe that the Son of God should lay down his life in our behalf?; 3. God has no unwanted children. He makes no mistakes and does not traffic in accidents. It is his cattle on a thousand hills and he knows his sheep by name.

The first man was called Adam. The first woman was called Eve. Our scripture tells us that God creates persons and they are called "precious;" creatures of *worth*.

Moreover, it also follows that we are *a people capable of assuming moral responsibility*. How much moral responsibility have we assumed when 1. our natural resources are being depleted at an alarming rate, 2. food surpluses are being destroyed while millions are starving, 3. the crime rate continues to soar and we already have more criminals than we have places to put them, 4. economically, our two main words are still 'profit' and 'me.' And there is another moral question which can no longer be put on the back burner. The question of what moral responsibility do we exercise related to nuclear weapons? It is no longer a question of "what if?" but of "what do we do now?" The hard facts are sobering:

> a. a twenty-megaton bomb contains the equivalent of twenty million tons of TNT, or five times the total energy of *all* the bombs dropped during World War II. By comparison, the Hiroshima bomb produced 13,000 tons of energy.
>
> b. a single such bomb would totally destroy every building and vaporize every person for a radius of six miles. Within twenty miles, persons would be killed instantly and every imaginable object would speed through the

air at 100 miles per hour. Over-pressure would burn and demolish everything.

c. persons up to twenty-six miles away would become instant flaming torches.

d. fire storms would be created for 3,000 square miles.

e. fall-out shelters would have the oxygen sucked from them, lethal fall-out would extend for thousands of square miles and radio-activity would linger for months or years.

That is *one* twenty-megaton bomb. This country presently has enough nuclear weapons to overkill every Russian forty times. Russia has the capacity to overkill every American twenty times. Again, "God had in wisdom created a people capable of assuming a moral responsibility." We no longer have the luxury of acting irresponsibly. A covenant binds both parties to certain obligations.

In Search of Self

A TELEVISION PROGRAM, *The People's Court,* currently enjoying a wide viewship involves a real-life judge presiding over actual courtroom cases. The judge sits behind the bench wearing a black robe, pronouncing final decisions pertaining to legal disputes. When you and I hear the term "judge," we probably envision such a person as the one just described. However, the judges described in the Old Testament functioned quite differently. Judges were military leaders who were raised up by the grace of God to govern Israel in times of trial. Psalm 2:10 relates that they enjoyed parallel authority to kings. It has been suggested that they were similar to the American Indian war chief whose authority was limited to the duration of a conflict.

The Hebrew people entered Canaan as a nomadic people with one God. Soon following the death of Joshua, it was as if they literally forgot themselves. Knowing little about agriculture, it was only natural that they should consult their Canaanite neighbors about how to manage crops. The Canaanites obliged not only by instructing them on how to raise crops, but also by teaching them about the gods who presided over the crops: the Baals. From that point on, things began to go downhill. The God who had brought them safely across the sea and the Jordan River was forgotten and the new Baals were worshipped. God's own people had literally forgotten who they were. The need was to get back to God.

From all appearances, it seems that from time to time we have forgotten our own identity. 1. *We have disillusioned ourselves into believing that we must have everything in small doses or condensed form. The Reader's Digest* has produced a condensed version of the Bible for those persons who "don't have the time" to read the Scriptures in their entirely. We attend speed-reading clinics to enable us to read faster, but then there are those who prefer to see a movie about something rather than read the book. We like our news in short snatches such as we find on the 6:00 or 10:00 news report. We take our meals from fast food outlets and often eat them on the run. We want our religion packaged neatly into an hour on Sunday morning, and if it goes beyond that, we begin shaking our watches. It is as if we believe we must have our food, news, entertainment, and religion in short doses. 2. *We have apparently fallen victim to a low self-esteem.* Robert Schuller has written a new book entitled *Self-Esteem: The New Reformation,* in which he proposes that the reason we are willing to settle for second and third best is because we have such a low opinion of ourselves. We will not pursue that observation here, but will simply remark that low self-esteem is a contradictory attitude to the picture of humanity presented in the Scriptures: "created in the image of God," and "the child of a king." 3. *We have embraced what I refer to as a placebo ethic.* That is, an ethic which is questionable but which makes us just "feel better" because we espouse it. Consider for instance, the movie rating system, which we have mistaken to be a kind of safeguard against our youth being offended by objectionable material (i.e., "PG" or "R" ratings). We know however, that any youth who has the price of admission can usually be admitted. We know that probably they are not going to hear any word that they have not already heard before. We know that they are not going to see much more violence than they have already seen on the 6:00 news. We know that about anything else they would see, they probably have seen it in some form or another already. We know that the rating is all but irrelevant, but we just "feel better" because it is there. We admonish our youth not to do something which we turn around and do ourselves, but we "feel better" because we have admonished them.

The Hebrew people in Canaan were faced with the problem of recovering their own identity. I submit, so are we!

One's Proper Service   Isaiah 58:3

I READ RECENTLY that a member of a United Methodist church in North Carolina was once convicted in court for disrupting church services because of his atrocious singing. It was in 1873 that William Linkhaw was hauled into county court in Robeson, N.C., by fellow Methodists who charged that Linkhaw's singing repeatedly created havoc during worship services. Not only was his voice offensive to the ear, but he was given to singing long after the rest of the congregation had stopped. Things had become so disconcerting that even the minister refused to sing. Consequently, Linkhaw was found guilty of a misdemeanor and ordered to remain silent in church. However, the state supreme court overturned the conviction, sympathetic to Linkhaw's claim that singing was a part of his service to God. I was interested in this particular item because I well remember when an old fellow in my home church was asked to surrender his choir robe on the same grounds. As a boy, it struck me as rather ridiculous that those of us in the choir, many of whom could not carry a tune in a wheelbarrow, should presume to single out Mr. X. After all, he was an affable gentlemen who had been a member of the choir for probably fifty years. He was not a person of means and not physically able to participate in the church's visitation program or serve on any committee. His days were spent sitting at home with his good wife who had been in poor health for as long as I could remember. He could however, do one thing for his church. He could manage to get away for a couple of hours on Sunday morning and sing in the choir. His service though, as precious as it was to him, was no longer appreciated. I suppose the rationale behind the choir's decision was the Mr. X's service was no longer "proper."

What is one's proper service to God? In Isaiah's day, the supreme service was considered to be "fasting." Widely practiced as a kind of personal purge and expression of humility, fasting was a common experience among the devout throughout the ancient world. The Israelites incorporated fasting in national religious life more prominently after Jerusalem fell to the Babylonians in 586 B.C. Unfortunately, the Jews mistook this particular gesture as a guarantee of spiritual righteousness; a kind of "automatic purification" which placed them blameless before God. Consequently, it was inconceivable to them that hardships would continue following their dedicated "service." When hardships would continue, they felt an explanation was in order: "Why have we fasted and thou seest it not? Why have we humbled ourselves, and thou takest no knowledge of it." (58:3) Listen to God's answer: "Behold, in the day of your fast you seek your own pleasure, and oppress all your workers. Behold, you fast only to quarrel and to fight and to hit with wicked fist. Fasting like yours this day will not make your voice to be heard on high." (58:3, 4) Their service was unacceptable. In a word, it was mechanical; in another word, it was self-serving. In still yet another word, it was presumptuous. The service which God seeks involves the extension of his love for others and in an attitude of praise. In the words of John Wesley, serving God means, "serving neighbors, whether they be friends or adversaries, doing good to every man and willingly hurting no man." Wesley practiced what he preached. He traveled about 225,000 miles, preached about 50,000 times to crowds small and large, often up to 20,000, occasionally facing hostile mobs and barrages of stone and mud. But he had a plucky, game spirit, going on to the next town, leaving his class and "bands" to multiply. The service of outreach performed by Wesley, even with our precise statistics and access to his faithfully kept journals, is measureless.

Isaiah scored the people of Israel for indulging in perfunctory rituals, mistaking them for "service." Instead, he laid down God's prescription for service: "to loose the bonds of wickedness, to undo the thongs of the yoke, to let the oppressed go free, and to break every yoke . . . to share your bread with the hungry, and bring the homeless poor into your house; when you see the naked, to cover him." (58:6-7)

William Linkhaw believed that a part of his service to God was to sing in the church choir. I am inclined to agree with him. His voice may have been off key, but his comprehension of service to God was not. What is your service to God?

A Mountain-Top Experience

OUR PRIMARY FOCUS will be upon the divine Sonship of Jesus of Nazareth. Notice that we say Jesus of "Nazareth" here instead of Jesus "Christ." Prior to the events which we shall take up, Jesus had been identified simply as "the Nazarene," "the carpenter," or "the carpenter's son." Following two specific events, his identity is enlarged upon to include "divine Sonship." What happened? There was a baptism and a transfiguration.

Baptism. The practice of baptism was not the peculiar invention of Christianity. Other religions, in fact, political systems, had long observed a form of "washing" or "sprinkling with water" as an initiatory act of accepting "outsiders" into their fellowship. John's baptism, insofar as it was the "baptism of repentance" (Mark 1:4), was distinguished from the others. He proclaimed that one mightier than himself soon would come whose baptism was still yet different than his: "I indeed have baptized you with water; but he shall baptize you with the Holy Ghost." (Mark 1:8) The difference is further realized in that there is no record of Jesus ever having baptized anyone with water. However, Jesus of Nazareth submitted himself for John's water baptism in order to 1. identify himself with John's message, 2. receive the public blessing of God through a symbolic act that all would understand, and 3. certify his divine Sonship. "And it came to pass in those days that Jesus came from Nazareth of Galilee, and was baptized of John in the Jordan . . . . and there came a voice from heaven, saying, 'Thou art my beloved Son, in whom I am well pleased.'" (Mark 1:9-11)

Transfiguration. Six days following the baptism, Jesus took Peter, James, and John and withdrew to the top of a mountain, possibly Mt. Hermon. There, he was "transfigured;" that is to say, in a moment of spiritual union with God the Father, his countenance was transformed. Even his garments became glistening, intensely white (Mark 9:3), and Moses appeared with Elijah to speak with him. A cloud, long identified with the presence of God, i.e., 'firey, cloudly pillar,' overshadowed them, and a voice spoke from the cloud; "This is my beloved son; listen to him." (Mark 9:7) Dramatically, the carpenter's son was now understood to be the "Son of God."

There is also one other noteworthy reference in our selected scripture. In Mark 9:5, James, Peter, and John wanted to erect three booths (or tabernacles) on a sacred spot and remain there in the afterglow. Moses had been tempted to do the same thing following his own mountaintop experience. However, it has always happened, it seems, that following high moments on a "mountain top," there is work to do in the valleys. To formalize a religious experience and not share it with others, or to interpret it through our lives, is to miss the point of the experience itself. Peter, James, and John built no shrine; they became living messages of the one to whom they said, "Truly, you are the Son of God." (Matthew 14:33)

The Force Acts 7:30-32

A HIGH SCHOOL graduating class in California omits the invocation from its proceedings because of a law suit brought by three seniors who claimed the brief prayers would violate the "separation of church and state" clause of the Constitution. This is but one instance, part of a long-growing list, to be contained in a manual that our generation appears to be authoring: "How to Dismiss God from the Universe." To whom or what shall we ultimately be driven? What was the *first* tiny spark in the abysmal darkness? The *first* cause? The *initial* force? How did the universe come into being? Was it the handiwork of a great "Whom it may concern," or the climax of a colossal cosmic chaos? Read no farther than the first verse of the Bible: "In the beginning God created the heavens and the earth."

I remember having once spent several days meticulously fitting together pieces of a jigsaw puzzle, only to have a leg under the card table collapse, dumping the puzzle all over the floor. It was one of those puzzles with a lot of autumn colors in it, and had been extremely difficult, if not exasperating to assemble. It would have been marvelous if I could have just sat down on the floor, gathered up all the scattered pieces, thrown the whole business up in the air and let them fall into their proper places on the floor. How many times do you think a person would have to throw the pieces in the air before they would finally come down fitted together to form the perfect picture? The chances of that ever happening are about as likely as the universe having "just accumulated" out of cosmic stuff, without design, without a creator.

All evidence, no matter how paltry, points to the same conclusion: the universe is *designed*! On the lowly end of the spectrum, the earthworms in an acre of soil can bring to the surface more than eighteen tons of earth. In twenty years, a new layer of topsoil three inches thick will have been created by *worms*,

65

which also fill the soil with holes, allowing air to circulate free-ly. On the other end of the spectrum, take into account that the farthest detectable star from earth is ten billion light years away. There are stars beyond that but not within the scope of our instruments. Inasmuch as *one* light year equals six tril-lion miles, imagine the distance to the star ten billion light years away, and appreciate the testimony of Psalm 19:1; ''The heavens are telling the glory of God; and the firmament proclaims his handiwork.''

IN ALL PROBABILITY, you know of some young boy who bears such a striking resemblance to his father that a person would know immediately, even in a crowd, that they were father and son. The father can be seen in the son. The Bible tells us that "God was Christ!" In what ways did the Son resemble the Father?

a. *In his life*. Jesus affirmed and celebrated life. His was not the attitude that this world and all that is in it are despicably evil . . . that the object is to totally reject life with an eye always on "glory" . . . that beauty in any form must be repressed as a tool of the devil. No, instead, Christ affirmed and celebrated life. Not a recluse, he enjoyed *friendships* with Lazarus, Mary, Martha, and others. He observed simple *domestic gestures* and was so impressed by them that he gave them a prominent place in his teachings (a woman sweeping a house, or drawing water at a well, baking bread, old wineskins bursting with new wine, lamps flickering in the night, patches on old garments). He enjoyed and absorbed the movements in *nature* and referred to them in order to illustrate his message; birds gathering into trees, foxes going into dens, figs withering, storm clouds boiling. Jesus affirmed life in such a positive manner, experiencing and relating to God's great intention and design for all he had made, that we may understand life is not to be either seized nor rejected, but "lived" in an attitude of "Praise God!" In the harmony of Christ's life with creation, we see something of God's great intention and design for each of us.

b. *In his ministry*. Jesus' ministry was characterized by the absolute "giving" of himself. He was, as one theologian puts it, "radically obedient" to God. In the same spirit, he was "radically giving" to others, always reaching, touching, healing, praying, searching, loving. The Bell Telephone Company did not originate the concept of "Reach Out and Touch

Someone." The concept was in the mind of God before creation and the practice is as old as Eden. It was perfected in Jesus Christ, proclaimed in the New Testament, and is as relevant today as this morning's newspaper. The ministry of Christ reveals a God who "spends" himself for creation

c. *In his teaching.* Jesus was able to recognize and relate to God in the common life through his teachings. His life, ministry, and teachings combined to reveal a God of boundless love, caring, concern, and sensitive compassion. What he taught, he practiced. Even in death he was consistent with the witness of his life. Having spoken of "forgiving one's enemies" and those who "despitefully use you," he gathered his words into action on Calvary. "Father, forgive them," he prayed. He taught so very much more, all of which was personified in his life. He showed that if the "good teacher" is flawlessly consistent, how much more consistent and loving must be our heavenly Father?

d. *In his resurrection.* Here, God unmistakably reveals himself. His power is beyond imagination. His *promises* are made good. His *intentions* and *purposes* will not be overthrown. His actual *involvement* in the world is confirmed. In the resurrected Christ, God is clearly revealed. God was, in all ways, in Christ!

Some Rules Need to be Broken

LET US FABRICATE a situation in order to refer to an actual circumstance. Suppose that your family doctor spent the better part of his time enjoying the company of his cohorts, all of them healthy, sharing a common interest, and preserving the clinic by keeping it in good repair, yet never associated with persons beset by maladies. The clinic has been the medical center for as long as anyone can remember, but is used primarily for research and as a place to house medical books. The doctors are far too involved with perusing the records, studying cures, and maintaining the dignity of medicine to bother themselves with the sick and infirm. To carry this hypothetical situation further, let us say that a new doctor appears in town, totally unrelated to the time-honored clinic, independent of the guild. He seeks out the diseased, actually associates with them, and proceeds to cure their ailments. Immediately, the professional guild begins to question his credentials and stirs up public opinion against him.

Now read Mark 2:15-17. Jesus has invited certain tax collectors and "sinners" to dinner in his own home. The scribes and Pharisees, no doubt chaffed because Jesus had not invited them instead, raised a question which is, in fact, unintelligible for men of their profession: "Why does he eat with tax collectors and sinners?" Why was he not at the holy of holies with them observing proper rituals and diet? Why did he not take his fellowship with the saints, the "clean" and righteous? Jesus not only explained the messianic format, he also reprimanded them for their insular hypocrisy: "Those who are well have no need of a physician, but those who are sick; I came not to call the righteous, but sinners."

The Pharisees were monitors of the Law. It is true . . . there must always be individuals around us to call our attention to the rules, but it is an additional gift of grace when such persons possess at least a minimum of common sense. Some years ago, I received a telephone call from a parishioner who desperately pleaded that I come immediately to her house and rush her to the emergency room of a local hospital. Knowing that she had been experiencing difficulty with her pregnancy, I did not ask questions, but quickly ran to the car and hurried to her house. She was waiting on the front porch as I drove into the driveway. As I helped her into the car, she kept saying, "Hurry, hurry!" In a matter of moments I drove up to the entrance of the emergency room, jumped from the car and started around to open the door to assist the young lady inside. Even before I could reach the other side of the car, a man in uniform came charging from behind the sliding glass doors shouting, "You can't park here . . . this area must be kept open for emergency!" I explained to him that this was an emergency. "I can't help that," he said, "you'll have to move the car before you can bring her in." I had to move the car, park it at a considerable distance from the emergency room entrance and almost carry the expectant mother into the hospital. As I mentioned, there must always be individuals to remind us of the rules, but it is an additional gift of grace if they have a minimum of common sense.

The Pharisees scolded Jesus for associating with sinners (Mark 2:16), chastized him for plucking grain for nourishment on the sabbath (23-28), and rebuked him for healing a man with a withered hand on the same day. (3:1-6) Jesus was threatening their security, their positions, and assuming their authority. Not surprisingly, rather than reassessing their own witness, they dug in all the more, and "stirred up the people against him."

Looking for Signs John 4:51-52

SEVERAL YEARS AGO I was a member of the Arkansas delegation which attended a jurisdictional seminar of some sort in Dallas, Texas. Our delegation included an exceptional Christian gentlemen, whose name you would probably recognize, just recently assigned as the Episcopal leader of the Arkansas Area. As a matter of fact, he had moved into the Episcopal residence only two weeks prior to the seminar. One evening as we filed slowly past a buffet table to fill our plates, I chanced to be behind two members of the conference from which the new bishop had come. One of the gentlemen nudged his companion, nodded toward the new bishop, and said under his breath, "Does he look like a bishop to you?" The companion continued to heap up his plate, smiled, and softly replied, "No way." Apparently, they saw no sign of authority in his gentle manner, no sign of dignity in his congeniality, no sign of spiritual aura about his unpretentious appearance. Brother, were they wrong!

Some people are always looking for signs. It is not a new thing under the sun. How many times do you suppose it was remarked behind Jesus' back, "Does he look like a messiah to you?" Joseph's son he was; a carpenter by trade, wearing a mother-made robe, keeping company with the blue-collar element, and stirring up everything that had been settled. Oh, there were signs all right . . . signs that he was in league with the Prince of Darkness: a miracle here, an exorcism there, taking liberty with the Scriptures, condemning the establishment. How could any rational person believe him? But rational people did believe him. What is more, many believed him *without* a sign. That is actually the emphasis of what we are about here . . . that he was believed *without* a sign.

1. The Gospel according to John tells us that many Samaritans believed in Jesus because of the testimony of the woman at the well. (4:7-30) However, let us hasten to verse 42; "They

said to the woman, 'It is no longer because of your words that we believe, for we have heard for ourselves, and we know that this is indeed the Savior of the world.'''

2. John further relates that when Jesus came to Capernaum, an official prevailed upon him to heal his son who was at the point of death. Jesus said, "Unless you see signs and wonders you will not believe." (v.48) The official impressed Jesus by answering, "Sir, come down before my child dies." (v. 49) In other words, without benefit of signs, the man already believed. Jesus rewarded the official's faith by saying, "Go; your son will live." (v.50) Now, take notice of the response: "The man believed the word that Jesus spoke to him and went on his way." (50) He believed *before* the sign. (4:51-53)

Is your belief contingent upon a sign? If so, what? A supernatural event, a special feeling, a bush of fire, or on the other hand, is your belief and faith in Christ operative beyond dependency upon signs?

Beyond Ambiguity Isaiah 42:1

IN THE 1500s, there lived a "prophet" named Nostradamus who upheld the Copernican theory that the world is round and circles the sun more than one hundred years before Galileo was prosecuted for the same belief. He was also widely known as a healer, a dabbler in the occult, and predictor of events far into the future. A present day book, *The Prophecies of Nostradamus*, purports to show that he predicted such specific events as the assassination of John F. Kennnedy, Hitler's rise to power, the Blockade of Britain, the Common Market, and other far sweeping events. The writings of Nostradamus are, however, exceedingly ambiguous, requiring a great deal of imagination on the part of the reader to even remotely apply them to events claimed as "fulfillments." I personally place no stock in this ancient mystic's poetic "prophecies." But there is no ambiguity in the prophecies of Isaiah: (1). "Behold my servant, whom I uphold, my chosen, in whom my soul delights; I have put my spirit upon him, he will bring forth justice to the nations." (42:1) Let us now turn to Matthew 3:16: "As soon as Jesus was baptized, he went up out of the water. At that moment heaven was opened, and he saw the Spirit of God descending like a dove and lighting on him. And a voice from heaven said, 'This is my son whom I love; with him I am well pleased."

The servant described in Isaiah 53 was to be (2). a suffering servant; "Surely, he has borne our griefs and carried our sorrows; yet we esteemed him stricken, smitten by God, and afflicted. But he was wounded for our transgressions, he was bruised for our iniquities; upon him was the chastisement that made us whole, and with his stripes we are healed." (vv. 4,5) The entire New Testament is testimony to the "Song of the Servant," and in the remarkable economy of God, the wounds and bruises resulted in inclusive wholeness and healing. Unfortunately, there are those who have not embraced the vicarious suffering Christ as relevant for their own cases. Even on Christmas day, combat raged in eastern El Salvador between government troops and leftist rebels. A Roman Catholic priest claims that nearly 7,000 persons died in "blind violence" in the country during the past year. We will not dwell upon world violence and political unrest here, except to say that there are those who remain outside of the peace made possible by the redemptive work of Christ. But for those who have experienced the power of Christ in their lives personally, they have found it to be a strong potion, even in difficult times.

Slightly more than one hundred years ago, an especially gifted young man enrolled in Glasgow University. Anxious to begin academic studies and anticipating his forthcoming marriage, his spirits soared. But how rapidly the wheels of fortune turn. He was suddenly stricken by blindness, and his fiance, not wanting to be married to an invalid, rejected him. The tide had turned against him in a manner which would have devastated a lesser person. However, despite his adversities, he graduated from the university and went on to become one of the greatest preachers in the Church of Scotland. Not out of his despair, but out of his personal relationship with Christ, he wrote a hymn which we lift in praise until this day: "O Love That Wilt Not Let Me Go . . ." Consequently, not only the New Testament, but individuals like George Matheson the hymnwriter and scores of others who have named the name of Christ, affirm that Isaiah's prophecy has indeed come to pass.

There is more. The vicarious suffering of Christ was (3). once done, for all, and for all time. Such a sacrifice need never be repeated. I have read where each year, beginning on Ash Wednesday, thousands of Filipino Christians begin Lenten observances by flagellating themselves with whips and heavy branches. The whips have sharp stones and broken pieces of glass affixed to leathered ends. Certain others submit themselves to be actually crucified. Their devotion is admirable, but the gestures in which they engage are both barbaric and unnecessary. We continue to sin, yes, but the redemptive work of Christ at Calvary endures, once done for all time.

The Mirror of Judas

SO MUCH has been written, discussed, and speculated about Judas that we feel we know enough about him already. And really, what more is there to say of him other than he is for all times the supreme symbol of betrayal? Nothing, unless we are willing to admit that there was such about his life which causes us to be introspective about our own.

1. *Jesus had confidence in him.* To begin with, Jesus observed qualities about Judas which were suitable for discipleship. Had there been no goodness, no promise, no ability, Judas certainly would not have been included among the Twelve. Moreover, he was capable and trustworthy enough to be selected as treasurer for the group. So for whatever reason, future potential or ability already acquired, Jesus had confidence in him.

Has not Christ placed tremendous confidence in us? The care of his church, the propagation of his message, the extension of his ministry, faithfulness to our vows. Shall we too betray his confidence?

2. *Judas knew how to be discerning.* He was not without practical judgment. The care of the treasury would hardly be entrusted to a reckless, emotion-driven individual. Judas was present in the house of Mary and Martha when Mary anointed the feet of Jesus with an expensive ointment. His protest of the anointing is not without merit, inasmuch as his concern was not for himself, but that the ointment could have been sold and the money given to the poor. From time to time a similar protest is raised today by those who question the wisdom of erecting church facilities costing hundreds of thousands of dollars while so many hungry remain to be fed.

Each of us has been entrusted with the freedom of choice and the ability to discern. Do we betray Christ by our choices?

3. *Judas had opportunity.* His position among Christ's chosen naturally enabled him to produce a positive witness.

And even near the end, he had the opportunity to abort his scheme, the motive of which is still unclear to us. Jesus announced at the table that the one who would betray him would dip in the same dish as the others. Judas played dumb, but inwardly he knew that Jesus saw through his pretense. Judas had opportunity.

As members of Christ's family, we have numerous opportunities to make positive witnesses. As a people who have followed our own schemes and well-devised plans, we have the opportunity to repent. Shall we betray Christ by bungling our opportunity?

4. *Judas had access to Jesus.* The fact that Judas was able to walk up to Christ in the garden and greet him with a kiss, the traditional greeting of a disciple for a teacher, clearly establishes that he had easy access to Jesus.

The Scriptures tell us that Christ serves as our "high priest," interceding on our behalf, having access to God, even as we have access to the Son through prayer. To neglect prayer and the spiritual life is to abuse the access. Shall we betray Christ by abusing our access?

What more is there to say of Judas, unless we are willing to admit that there was such about his life which causes us to be introspective about our own?

Evil in the Trenches   Mark 11:15-18

IN CONSIDERATION of our scripture selection, the title as listed above appears to be unreasonably over-stated. In our mind's eye, we conceive Jesus and the disciples striding directly into a well-laid trap. The priests are hunkering low in waist-deep trenches, the scribes located strategically in reinforced bunkers, their religious peers dug in somewhere behind barbed wire barricades . . . "entrenched evil." But no, it was not to be that obvious. Evil entrenches itself in many ways. We will mention here some of the more glaring entrenchments encountered by Jesus and the twelve as they entered the holy city.

1. *Corruption.* Dishonesty, misrepresentation, and crookedness are always evil because they are the manifestation of a lie. Corruption had carried over onto the temple steps. The money-changers were short-changing alien Jews who had come to purchase sacrifical animals for the Passover. Those who sold pigeons were receiving top dollar while peddling inferior merchandise. The temple area had been transformed into a carnival atmosphere. Not surprisingly, Jesus "began to drive out those who sold and those who bought in the temple, and he overturned the tables of the moneychangers and the seats of those who sold pigeons." (11:15)

2. *Prejudice.* The institutional luminaries, the priests and religious authorities, would have none of the revolutionary carpenter's blasphemies occur in their jurisdiction if they could prevent it. Immediately, they took up their favorite ploy of setting the people against him. Moreover, in self-righteous arrogance, they accosted him with loaded questions. (11:27-33) Prejudice is entrenched evil, no matter of its object.

3. *Fear.* The scriptures say the chief priests and scribes "feared" him. Fear causes one to imagine things and dig in at the heels, creates paranoia, and circles the wagons around defenses. Fear entrenches. Jesus encountered corruption, prejudice, and fear upon entering the holy city.

77

4. *Brokenness*. Brokenness is evil because it disintegrates and prevents wholeness. Jesus came to heal physical, spiritual, mental, and social brokenness. This had been his ministry for three turbulent years, but he had not eliminated it; Jerusalem was evidence of that.

Jesus indeed confronted "entrenched evil." As Christians, we are called apart to continue the confrontation.

Appointment in Jerusalem

SEVERAL YEARS AGO I saw a rather celebrated movie which had ambitiously undertaken to portray the life of Christ. Although the larger part of the film left a great deal to be desired, at least one scene was, for me, worth the price of admission. Jesus and his disciples were on their way to Jerusalem, passing along the edge of the sea. The face of Jesus was stern, his jaw set, and his eyes fixed straight ahead. The same camera receded until it brought into focus the disciples, the sky, the expanding shoreline, and Jesus . . . striding ahead of the others, like a man about to be late for an appointment. I have often recalled that scene, believing that it was with just such urgent resolve that Jesus and his disciples were "going to Jerusalem." As elementary as they may appear, two other things ought to be noted regarding the actual "going;"

1. *It was Jesus' decision.* That is to say, he *chose* to go. Characters on stage recite a script, robots manuever as they are programmed, and puppets are manipulated by someone jerking on a string. Real people make *decisions*. Jesus did not go to Jerusalem simply because it had been written down for him to do so centuries before . . . a character reading his lines, being jerked around by a cosmic puppeteer. How primitive it is to reduce Jesus to a wind-up messiah or a "throw-away" person by insisting that he had no mind of his own regarding his own ministry. He *chose* to go to Jerusalem.

2. *It was a decision which would cost his life.* He was aware of this even as he made the decision. When someone is led toward a calculated death, it is called a "killing." When someone willingly lays down his life, it is referred to as a "sacrifice." Notice, the Bible speaks of a sacrifice, not a killing.

Luke 19:29-35. Use your imagination for a moment. You are sitting leisurely in your den enjoying precious time with your family when suddenly you hear a disturbance on the

79

carport. You rush to the door, peer curiously outside, and discover two strange men attempting to remove your car from the carport. Quickly, you spring outside demanding an explanation. Their explanation: "We're taking your car, the Lord needs it." What would be your reaction? Would their explanation satisfy you? Apparently such an explanation was adequate for the owners of the colt referred to in the passage, for no other conversation is recollected. How do you explain the ease with which the two disciples simply walked away with someone else's property.

Luke 19:37-38. One other matter for consideration: Verse 37 relates that as Jesus rode the colt at the descent of the Mount of Olives "the multitude" rejoiced and praised God. The multitude? Who were they? Where did they come from? How did they know to be there at that particular time? How did they associate the man on the colt with the messiah?. (read Zechariah 9:9 and Psalm 118:26-27)

The "going up" to Jerusalem was the result of a monumental personal *decision*, a decision which would *cost the life of Jesus*, and involved considerable *faith* on the part of many.

FOR THREE WEEKS the minister announced in the church newsletter that a called meeting of the Administrative Board would be held to consider enlarging the church kitchen. For three weeks, the same announcement appeared in the Sunday worship bulletin and was repeated verbally from the pulpit. On the appointed date, the board met, deliberated the details, and voted to move ahead with the kitchen project. Construction was soon under way. One morning, a member of the board happened by the church and was curious to know what all the commotion was about in the kitchen. It was explained that the kitchen was being enlarged. The board member was irate. "Who authorized that?" he demanded. He was informed that the Adminsitrative Board had met and unanimously approved the project. "Why didn't I know anything about the meeting?" he snapped hatefully. That was a good question, considering he had been in church each Sunday the announcement was made and the newsletter had carried the same information into his home for three successive weeks. Why do people not pay attention? Are they (we) preoccupied, disinterested, along for a free ride, or just simply contrary? For whatever reason, it is both disconcerting and annoying to be ignored repeatedly.

Jesus and his disciples were on their way to Jerusalem and, in what was actually his third announcement of his approaching death, Jesus said: "Behold, we are going up to Jerusalem; and the Son of man will be delivered to the chief priests and the scribes, and they will condemn him to death, and deliver him to the Gentiles; and they will mock him, and spit upon him, and scourge him, and kill him; and after three days he will rise." (10:33-34) James and John, the sons of Zebedee, had not heard a word of it! Immediately, their ambitions, which doubtless they had been stroking while Jesus had been speaking, came to the front. En route to a human sacrifice, they dared to ask for places of honor in the kingdom. (10:37)

They were indeed, as the writer of the hymn, "Are Ye Able?" describes them — sturdy dreamers.

Jesus taught that to seek places of honor is to be off on the wrong trail; service is the objective. "The Son of man also came not to be served but to serve, and to give his life as a ransom for many." (10:45)

In the Eleventh Hour   Mark 14:32-36

SEVERAL YEARS AGO, Dr. Claude Thompson, distinguished member of the faculty at Candler School of Theology in Atlanta, received the report from a team of physicians that he had only a short time to live. Each day, each moment, became precious to him. No movement was without meaning, and his words were chosen carefully. He knew he was going to die. There were some things he wanted to say to his students and colleagues, and in a heroic act of eleventh-hour witness, he addressed the seminary community. As a man on his way to a certain death, he wanted to be sure that some essential things were laid down before his departure. When the time is short, only essentials matter.

Jesus was to have only a few short hours with his disciples. He knew it. The shadow of the cross was lengthing, and in three particular portions of Mark's fourteenth chapter, we observe three familiar incidents which will forever remain in our memories as pertaining to our Lord's last meeting with the twelve. Strangely enough, each of them touches upon loyalty.

1. *14:22-25*. There was the Passover meal which Jesus dramatically transformed into a messianic banquet which we have come to know as the "Lord's Supper." Let us assume all the symbolisms and transitions of this meal in order to hurry on to say that the meal was a call to loyalty. "Do this in rememberance of me," he said. "Continue this sacrament," he urged so that the coals of ministry would not burn low in his absence. Early Christians observed the sacrament several times daily. Today, some communions partake of the elements each Sunday, others each first Sunday of the month, and still others quarterly. The fact that the sacrament was considered as an "essential" ought to challenge us to rethink our own loyalty to it.

2. 14:29-31. Here we encounter Peter's false loyalty, his claim that even though all others would fall away, he would remain loyal. The Scriptures betray him, for we see him later squirming uncomfortably around an unfriendly fire, praying that no one would recognize him. Three times he denied Christ after swearing absolute loyalty. When the last record shall be tallied, the essential concern will be how loyal we were to Christ.

3. 14:32-36. "Remove this cup from me," Jesus prayed in the garden; alone, broken-hearted . . . knowing that all too soon the shadows would come alive with figures who would jerk him away for a final charade. But let us finish Jesus' prayer; "Remove this cup from me; yet not what I will, but what thou wilt." Radical loyalty, absolute obedience. In the shadow of the Cross, we see the essentials emerging. Loyalty is one. Can you name others?

The Last Meal

PERHAPS you have visited the Upper Room Chapel in Nashville, Tennessee, and had the opportunity to meditate before the marvelous wood carving and its appointments which so dramatically depict the Last Supper. One of the mysterious features of this particular carving is that no matter where you kneel before the figure of Christ, his eyes gaze strangely into yours. So it must have seemed to the disciples gathered around the table in Jerusalem on that fateful evening. How much more intense it must have been for Judas, and we can but wonder where his eyes were fixed when Jesus uttered those terrible words. "He who has dipped his hand in the dish with me, will betray me." (Matthew 26:23)

So far as the disciples were concerned, they had gathered, as they had done since childhood, to partake of the traditional Passover meal. The streets of Jerusalem were crowded with pious Jews who had come into the city for this express purpose. The ritual was always the same: while at the table, the story of the escape from Egypt would be recounted . . . there would be special foods on the table and unleavened bread would be eaten as a reminder of the haste in which the Exodus people had been forced to flee Egypt . . . it was always the same.

To the disciples' surprise however, Jesus suddenly departed from the familiar references; "And he took bread, and gave thanks, and broke it, and gave unto them saying, 'This is my body which is given for you: this do in remembrance of me.' Likewise also the cup after supper saying, 'This cup is the new testament in my blood, which is shed for you.'" Jesus had dramatically transformed the Passover supper into the Lord's Supper on the evening of his "last supper" with them. (see also Mark 14:22-24 and Matthew 26:26-29)

The Lord's Supper:

1. *Is a sacrament,* meaning that it was instituted by Christ and commanded to be continued "till he come." In Paul's familiar passage, used in the sacrament ritual, he adds, "For as often as ye eat this bread and drink this cup, ye proclaim the Lord's death till he comes." (1 Corinthians 11:26)

2. *Symbolizes the new covenant.* The Old Testament covenant of the Law was sealed with the blood of animal sacrifice. However, this covenant had failed. The prophets themselves had said, "Behold, the days will come, saith Jehovah, that I will make a new convenant with the house of Israel, and with the house of Judah." The covenant of Law was being superseded by the new convenant of love, sealed by the blood of Christ.

3. *Uses of common elements.* In addition to using the traditional elements of the Passover, bread and wine, Jesus realized that each day when his followers partook of their meals, two things were certain to be on the table . . . bread and wine. Consequently, even an ordinary meal would include reminders of the new covenant.

4. *Was observed anxiously.* Devout early Christians met daily to observe the sacrament in the prayerful hope that Jesus would return while they were sharing the sacred meal. In time, the early Church observed the sacrament each Sunday, a practice continued until the Reformation. Oddly enough, in Scotland, during the sixteenth century, it was observed in the country twice and in town four times a year.

5. *Is called the eucharist,* meaning the "thanksgiving," based on the passage, "He took a cup, and when he had given thanks . . ."

Perhaps John Calvin spoke for each of us when he admitted that "the matter is too sublime for me to be able to express, or even to comprehend . . . I rather experience it, than understand it."

What Kind of Cross?   Mark 8:34

NOT LONG AGO, a hard-rock singer reknowned for his notorious over indulgence in mind-altering drugs appeared on television to scream, lunge, and gyrate through one of his best-selling songs. Inasmuch as the rather badly garbled words were totally incomprehensible to me, I turned my attention to the bizarre, uninhibited attire of this widely heralded "artist." Not to dwell on the flamboyance of his appearance, I wish only to point out that dangling from an expensive chain around his neck was a large cross. Perhaps it was there as a counter-statement, a message of rebellion to institutional religion, or perhaps he simply counted it as an attractive piece of jewelry. I do not know. But more and more, the cross is appearing on necklaces, earrings, bracelets, and the like as fashionable symbols, which is all right, I suppose, except that the behavior of those brandishing them is not always consistent with what the cross represents. If a person in ancient Rome had adorned himself with a cross, it would have been the equivalent of someone today wearing the likeness of the electric chair around his neck. The cross was originally not considered to be a thing of beauty. It conveyed pain, humiliation, and death. It still does, except in the Christian context. Another dimension was added to Calvary . . . *victory*.

Jesus issued a call to discipleship, but the invitation contained an inherent inhibitor: "If any man would come after me, let him deny himself and take up his cross and follow me." A cross of adornment or embellishment was not what Jesus had in mind. Self-denial and risking the consequences of following the way of Christ are at the heart of the call to discipleship.

In the eighteenth century, a German artist, Stenberg, was walking through the market place of his home town when he was attracted to the face of a dancing gypsy girl. He invited her to sit for him in his studio as a model. Accepting his

87

invitation, she enabled Stenberg to paint his famous "Dancing Gypsy Girl." There is more. The young girl was greatly impressed by what she saw in the artist's studio, particularly a painting in progress entitled "Crucifixion." Arrested by the painting, she said one day to Stenberg, "He must have been a very bad man to have been nailed to a cross like that." Stenberg replied, "No, he was a good man. The best man who ever lived. Indeed, he died for all men." The girl asked, "Did he die for you?" Stenberg had never really made such a personal application of his explanation. He was led to search the Scriptures, and in a few short weeks, he discovered the answer and surrendered himself to Christ. Returning to his painting of the "Crucifixion," he added these words beneath the likeness of Christ on the cross: "This I did for thee; what hast thou done for me?" There is more. A young aristocratic count, Zinzendorf by name, chanced to observe the painting, paused to meditate at both the depiction and the words, and was so moved that he went on to found the Moravians.

There are elements of power and attraction about the cross. There also is an inaudible appeal: "This I did for thee; what hast thou done for me?" Have we denied ourselves and taken up our cross, whatever it may be, and followed him?

And Their Eyes
Were Opened

SOME YEARS AGO, a movie entitled *Zapata* depicted the engaging story of the famous Mexican hero, Zapata. He was to the Mexicans what "El Cid" was to the Spanish: a redeemer of his people. Those who loved Zapata were radically devoted to him and his cause. At the end, when Zapata was ambushed by government troops, the white horse upon which he had led countless charges, escaped into the hills. The peasants violently refused to believe that their leader would have allowed himsef to be ambushed and killed, and whenever they caught a glimpse of the white horse in the hills, they claimed that it carried Zapata, signaling to them that he would return. They fully expected the return, but in time, the expectation died.

Although Jesus attempted on several occasions to interpret specific events to his disciples, as well as to prepare them for his certain return, not one of them was prepared. As Carlyle Marney once said, none of them lay hidden in the shrubbery near the tomb . . . waiting . . . waiting. Judas had gone off somewhere and hanged himself. The others were scattered, afraid, stroking their wounds, trying to recover from the total collaspe of everything. They had not been prepared for the crucifixion, much less the Resurrection. The post-Resurrection appearances mentioned in our scripture caught them totally by surprise. Two observations about the particular appearance described in our text:

1. The two men were on their way to Emmaus, discussing events pertaining to the crucifixion. Jesus caught up to them in the midst of their own journey, becoming a part of it himself, and in the end, baptizing it with his blessing. Those of us in the church believe that this is still the way Christ often comes into our lives. Off on our own journeys, pursuing some goal or objective, totally submerged in our own concerns . .

determined, ambitious, outrunning the spiritual life while in full stride toward that which we hope to achieve. And then, it happens. In half-step we are arrested by the sudden awareness of another presence; we had not expected it, nor do we always recognize it immediately. It just abides, and just as with the Emmaus travelers, it comes into clearer focus in due time. As the Holy Spirit accompanies us in our own journeys, it is hoped that somewhere along the way it may be with us as it was with them; "And their eyes were opened and they recognized him." (v. 31)

2. It is significant that Jesus was made known to them in the "breaking of bread." In the upper room Jesus had taken the elements of the Passover meal and transformed them into something completely different. The familiar ritual was changed from remarks about the Passover to references to the "body and blood" of the host. In a very real sense, Jesus' messianic identity was uniquely made known to them in the breaking of bread in the upper room. Then, at Emmaus, he was again "made known" in the breaking of bread. There are other references to post-Resurrection appearances of Jesus at which his presence was made known around a meal. (see Mark 16:14; John 21:9-14) Little wonder that early Christians quickly associated a mystical significance with the meal, more specifically, the Eucharist. Consequently, the church observed communion several times daily with the prayer, "Maranatha" (Come Lord!)

The expected return of Zapata was never fulfilled, and eventually the expectation faded. The unexpected return of Jesus of Nazareth took even his followers by surprise. Ironically, it seems that he must still catch us from behind.